Ulric Dahlgren

MEMOIR

OF

ULRIC DAHLGREN.

BY HIS FATHER,

REAR-ADMIRAL DAHLGREN.

" Pure from all stain, save that of human clay,
Which Christ's atoning blood hath washed away;
By mortal sufferings now no more oppressed,
Mount, sinless spirit, to thy destined rest!
While I, reversed our nature's kindlier doom,
Pour forth a father's sorrows on thy tomb."

PHILADELPHIA:
J. B. LIPPINCOTT & CO.
1872.

THIS MEMOIR

TO THOSE

UNION PRISONERS HELD AT RICHMOND,

FOR WHOSE LIBERATION FROM A CAPTIVITY

WORSE THAN DEATH,

ULRIC DAHLGREN

FREELY GAVE HIS OWN LIFE.

The death of Admiral Dahlgren prevented the realization of his earnest desire to contribute to the historic vindication of his heroic son Ulric, by the publication of this memoir. Consequently, this sad yet pleasing duty devolves upon his widow.

INTRODUCTION.

THE following sketch is designed to preserve the memory of one whose light was extinguished before the first year of manhood was completed, and whose ray glittered amid the noontide splendor with which the warriors of the Union emblazoned the standard of their glorious cause.

He laid down his young life, with all its bright promise, in a fruitless but noble effort to rescue his fellow-soldiers from the loathsome dungeons of the rebel capital.

So young!—and yet it seemed that riper years, even if extended to the utmost limit of the mortal term, were not needed to complete the evidences of honor, valor, purity, and devoted patriotism that irradiated the dawn of life.

The materials for this memoir have been found, partly in the personal recollection of the family, partly in his letters and little memoranda which he made occasionally; sometimes in the correspondence of the press, and in official documents. Much is unavoidably wanting that would have been of great interest, and so far this sketch is incomplete, though enough remains to establish fully the character and conduct of this youthful soldier.

While endeavoring to give some idea of the part that fell to his share in the great events of the time, it has been indispensable to sketch those events sufficiently to show his connection therewith. But in doing so, it has not been intended to trench on the province of history, or to take part in any of the professional questions that have arisen in regard to the conduct of military operations.

CONTENTS.

CHAPTER VII.

CHAPTER VIII.

CHAPTER IX.

CHAPTER X.

CHAPTER XI.

CHAPTER XII.

CHAPTER XIII.

MEMOIR

OF

ULRIC DAHLGREN.

CHAPTER I.

EARLY LIFE.

ULRIC DAHLGREN, the second son of Rear-Admiral and Mary Dahlgren, was born April 3d, 1842, at a rural home near the Neshamony, in Bucks County, Pennsylvania, where he received the first rites of the church from the hands of the Rev. J. P. Wilson, who little thought at the time that it would become his duty afterwards to bestow the last tribute of a friend and a Christian minister upon the mortal remains of this infant, then ripened to manhood and to a place in his country's remembrance.

When little more than a year old, his parents removed to Wilmington, Delaware, where he passed five years of happy childhood under the eye of a lovely and affectionate mother, upon whom the sole charge not unfrequently rested during the absence of her husband in the discharge of his professional duties.

He is well remembered as a laughing, sprightly little fellow, brimming with health and high spirits. In due course of time he passed from the white slip of infancy to the coveted honors of jacket and trousers. Memory recalls him seemingly very thoughtful in the grave contemplation of such an event, being one of the few moments, perhaps, when his merry features yielded to serious impressions.

Every accessory to the fullest indulgence of his juvenile activity might be found in the snug, cosy home, which was just fitted for the high place and holiday of children; their happiness unmarred by the fear of spoiling carpets or furniture. And there, at any time in the day, might be seen and heard little Ully, with his rosy, laughing face,—chirping and galloping around, whip in hand, making terrible commotion among imaginary horses and wagons in the shape of stools and chairs; while near by sat a fond mother, glancing now and then from needle and work towards her boy thus engaged; or, perhaps, when sorely worsted by the sport, demurely poring over his slate, with pencil in hand, limning uncouth but violently active figures, which, to his eye, took the shape of living animals of every description.

Thus rolled on the course of time, gradually developing both body and mind.

When six years of such life had been completed, the scene shifted,—for the duties in which the father was then engaged withdrew him so much from home that it became imperative to remove the family to a more convenient location.

So the happy little flock was gathered up, with as much of the home as was portable, and borne to Washington, which, from that time, became the residence of the family,—this was in May, 1848. And thus little Ully was transplanted to the national capital, where the remainder of his short but glorious life was to be passed, and to receive its future form and direction.

Two or three years were permitted to go by before the trammels of school-life were imposed, and these were uncheckered by events, save those which ordinarily pertain to juvenile life.

But the instincts of his nature, as subsequently recognized, were beginning to crop out,—particularly that fond attachment to horses which remained to the last. It is remembered that when taken to gratify his childish wonder by a sight of a new President, but an old warrior,* his quick response to the questions of the general was, "Where is Whitey?" for in his boyish estimation the horse

* General Taylor.

was as great as the rider that he had carried to battle, and most happy was he made by permission to see the illustrious quadruped.

At last came the school; and under the faithful teaching of that able scholar, Mr. O. C. Wight, Ully was initiated into the mysteries of Latin grammar, and the usual course of other branches.

Meanwhile many surrounding influences were at work, silently, gradually moulding the character.

At home, there was regularity and comfort, without ostentation; at school, steady, firm, conscientious instruction; while at both home and school, all due regard was paid to the religious training.

The intervals of study were spent with his father at the "ordnance department" of the Navy Yard,—where might be seen material of war in every variety, from its first inception to the finished cannon. Each nook of workshop and magazine was known to the boy,—he witnessed the silent labors of thought in his father's study, and their development in design; afterwards the elaborate finish of the accomplished draughtsman;* the arrangement of each part for the lathe or the vice by the busy, skillful foreman;† the glowing glories of the furnace, and the never-ceasing hum of the machinery, as the industrious and unrivaled workmen reduced the metal to its just proportions and finish. At

---

* Mr. Cluss. † Mr. Halroyd.

the battery, he gazed with deep interest on the hardy seamen, as they whirled onward the light howitzers with well-trained arms, or manned the ponderous cannon; then the stunning blast, the whir of the missile, and its quick flash as it burst far away, aimed at the distant mark. Around him was every contribution that invention or labor could give to the subject,—he heard discussed and saw tried every species of cannon and small arms, shot, shell, fuses, etc. that disciplined thought or wild fancy could devise; while his keen eye and sober thought were noting all and working out their own conclusions, so that, when afterwards launched upon the field of action, his judgment and experience in artillery were perceived and duly estimated by his superior officers.

His fondness for athletic exercises also found ample opportunity at the Navy Yard, where much of his leisure was passed in swimming and rowing, under the instruction of some of the ordnance seamen,—veterans these, fine specimens of a manly calling, who had been selected to serve there by reason of their experience or intelligence,—true lovers of boyhood, and ever ready to join in its pursuits or its pleasures. Under such tuition, Ulric became an expert swimmer and boatman.

Other influences, too, were at hand. Under the lofty domes of the Capitol, the school-boy often lingered to look upon the deliberations of the people's representatives. There he listened to the massive sentences of Webster and the graceful oratory of Clay, with bursts of eloquence and of thought from other powerful speakers.

The picture was filled in with occasional glimpses of Scott and other veteran warriors, whose achievements were recorded in his school-books, while the navy was represented by Morris, and Warrington, and Shubrick, and Smith, the relics of 1812.

Such mighty lights and shadows were not lost on the young intelligence, but were keenly regarded and well appreciated,—they could not but expand and elevate the mind, the heart, and the soul of the American youth.

He was only a little playful urchin when the events of 1850 had wellnigh ripened into catastrophe and hurried to fierce action those elements which, some ten years later, were to menace the existence of the Union, and to light the flame of a civil war in which he himself was destined to play his part and to close his earthly career.

Sorely puzzled were the boy and his brother to comprehend how professed friends to the country could approach its destruction so nearly; for the wild declamation of disloyal men, and an unreasoning portion of the press, were inflaming the common mind to madness, and it was no easy task for the master-spirits to rule the tempest.

The Whig leaders seemed to him identified with

the true doctrine, whilst his brother was inclined to the Democratic faith,—so the notions of the two school-boys often came into controversial collision. On one occasion, having exhausted their arguments and their breath, appeal was made to the father, who told them that both creeds were designed for the common good, dissimilar as they seemed; but, as disunion was now openly proposed as the only possible remedy, they were earnestly cautioned to beware of any political dogmas that tolerated such an idea, and to withdraw from all who countenanced it. This injunction, often repeated, is supposed by the father to have exercised a lasting influence on his son's convictions.

About this time, a very striking characteristic was the intense earnestness with which he pursued an object when once engaged in it; if he studied, it was not so much with the abstraction of a student as with the resolution to accomplish a set purpose,—while mixing in boyish sports he was just as intent,—nor was he less steadfast in adhering to a friend. It seemed as if he obeyed by instinct the scriptural injunction, "*Whatever thy hand findeth to do, do it with all thy might.*"

Ulric had entered upon his thirteenth year when the first pang of bitter sorrow was brought home to his young heart,—the mother that loved him so fondly, and had watched so tenderly over his early life, departed. She was one who, to every charm of rare beauty and a lovely presence, added the attractive graces of refined social life, and a Christian piety that never failed to win the admiration of her friends and the affectionate attachment of her family.

On this sad occasion, it was observed that he never left his father, who chose constantly to continue near the remains of one so cherished. There sat the dear boy, bowed in silent grief, utterly regardless of all passing objects. He felt there was good reason for sorrow, for he had lost a devoted mother, who had been faithful to every want,—in sickness or trouble her own hand ministering to his necessities, while by her precept and example the child knew what it was to pray, and to fail not in Sunday-school or in church. Her parting words deepened these impressions, and her last bequest to him was a Bible.

Thus life was rolling on in successive years, and the youth was growing into the form and thought of after-life, while the cultivation of his mind was not neglected, but was properly cared for. Yet it was plain that the bent and scope of the lad's nature found their end in ACTION. Where others thought, he seemed to think and act concurrently.

When about fourteen years of age, he and his elder brother accompanied their father on a trip on board the Merrimac, the first of a new class of steam-frigates, which had been completed, and which became so famous afterwards as the converted rebel iron-clad.

The armament was new, like the ship, and after the plans of his father, whose purpose it was to witness the first operation of the battery, and to offer such suggestions as might be needed. It was just such an occasion as boys would enjoy to the utmost, welcomed as they were in every part of the great ship, from forepeak to cabin, with that kindly heartiness which every sailor, whether officer or man, extends to a true boy; and no one of them all gave a more cordial greeting than the honest and gallant gentleman who commanded the ship, —Commodore Pendergrast.

The course of Ulric's life, as just sketched, underwent no change, save in the absence of his father, who went to sea in command of the United States ship Plymouth, and was agreeably surprised, while ascending the Potomac on his return, by an unexpected visit from Ulric. He had heard that the ship was in the river, and had lost no time in persuading some of his friends (the ordnance tars) to row him down, in order to meet the Plymouth, which he succeeded in doing not far from Mount Vernon. And when, a few months later, the ship put to sea to assist in checking the ill-judged interference of the British cruisers with our merchant vessels in the West Indies, Ulric accompanied his father, as far as he was allowed, down the river.

In the summer of 1858 his last term of schooling was completed. He was now well grounded in Latin and mathematics, as well as other branches usually taught,—and was a very promising draughtsman. Not that his father would have had his studies terminate at so early an age, but he discerned such unmistakable symptoms of distaste to further confinement to scholastic pursuits, and such eagerness to put in practice results already acquired, that he yielded to the boy's wishes, and consented that he should begin to fit himself for the vocation he was to follow. Upon full consideration of his son's tendencies, it was decided that this vocation was to be civil engineering and the law; and the Northwest was to be chosen for the exercise of these pursuits.

As a preparatory step, the rest of 1858 was passed in reviewing previous studies in field surveying, during which Ulric received practical instruction from his father in the use of the theodolite and plane-table.

With a view to further practice, he accepted an invitation from his uncle to visit the Southwest, where some tracts of wild land, which the latter possessed, afforded excellent opportunity to the student for a better acquaintance with his vocation.

In January, 1859, the lad set out from home, with a merry party of young cousins, the course of travel taking them through Richmond, where they arrived in the afternoon. His letter announcing this now lies before the writer of these lines. It is dated from the Exchange Hotel, and describes what he saw in walking around the town,—the State capitol, its senate-chamber, the statue of Washington, and other prominent objects. Little did the brave boy dream, as he traversed the streets of the Virginia capital, that a few short years would see him reappear on that scene, bringing with his charging squadrons hope to imprisoned comrades and terror to rebel councils,—then his own lifeless body would be borne along, perchance just where he trod, with every mark of indignity that panic-stricken traitors could offer, and destined by them to be forgotten in some nameless spot.

Yet events were rapidly hurrying the terrible drama into action.

A few more days of travel carried the party to the end of their journey.

For more than a year young Ulric gratified his ardent love for a life less trammeled by conventionalities than that of a city, and enjoyed the privilege of passing his leisure time in the solitudes of the forest and the plain; every faculty braced by breathing the free air of heaven, and by gazing upon the unstinted luxuriance of Nature in her most gorgeous display. At such times his horse and rifle were often his sole companions,—distances were spanned by the fleet hoofs of the one, while the other, wielded by a ready hand and a quick eye, found fitting mark as the nimble deer bounded by.

Here the youth found the school for the scout and the bivouac, that trained him in after-life to encounter Nature in her roughest as in her more pleasant moods.

In such pursuits he became familiar with the noble animal that so often bore him over every obstacle, and acquired such proficiency in his management as to make him one of the best riders of the day.

In looking over the simple events of this life, as disclosed by his own letters, it will be seen that he did not give himself up solely to the pleasures of the chase, but that he participated in the more plodding but useful labors of the plantation. At one time he is engaged in running lines, or laying out tracts of land, or repairing levees, or arranging papers for his uncle; then he has his studies, also, among which he appears much interested in improving himself in French.

Perhaps the plantations are remote from each other, and a ride of fifty miles and back makes a pleasant change to vary the drudgery. Perhaps a deer or a bear strays across the path, and agreeably puts an end to the thought that has lasted just long enough, or a stream may intersect the road to give interest to the journey. On one occasion he writes, "I tried to cross a bayou two hours ago, on Charley's horse, and when I had got half-way over he sank right down from under me, so I had to strike out and swim for shore," etc.

Then he inquires of his father in regard to ordnance matters, and is anxious to know something of each question as it arises,—of the gun of Armstrong, or of any other prominent inventor. He notices that a sixty-four pounder had burst and killed two of his old sailor friends; which grieves him. Sometimes he ventures an opinion on events elsewhere, such as the war in Italy, etc.

But the season wears around when more or less sickness prevails, and he is obliged to leave with the family for better air. He amuses himself with fencing, and French, and ten-pins; but so much relaxation does not comport with his earnest nature and industrious habits. He is soon to "*return to the hard work again which he prefers to all the rest.*" He writes, "*When I have nothing to occupy my mind, I always feel dissatisfied until I find myself busy again.*" And he contrives to find some employment even in this season, when exemption from exertion is considered admissible on account of the excessive heat: "*I have been busy the last week surveying a large avenue which will run through the woods.*"

Soon afterwards he returns to the plantation, and

writes in his usual cheerful and straightforward style. He is engrossed as before, running lines, surveying, etc.; goes at some length into details of a technical difficulty which he desires to know more of. Then he is engaged in hunting with his cousin. And so the year 1859 closes upon the young lad.

The next year opens with the glad notes of a wedding near his uncle's residence, in the pleasure of which he joins with his accustomed heartiness; but forgets not to send wishes to his own home that the coming year may be happy to all.

Again he is following the chase, and writes that the party "killed four deer,—his cousin two, and he two." Then he has a little adventure. In crossing a small lake his mare seemed to fail at the bank, and floundered in the soft mud. The moment was critical. Promptly the lad swung himself into the branches of an overhanging tree, and with one hand fired his piece close over the animal's head. Relieved of the rider's weight, and terrified by the sudden discharge, the animal bounded with desperate leap from the dangerous situation, cleared the bank, and made for home.

At this time he says that he is five feet ten and a half inches high, and weighs one hundred and thirty-six pounds.*

---

* Seventeen years and nine months old.

And now the youth, conscious of some ability to meet the vicissitudes of active life, makes known to his father his desire to try his own way in the world. He writes that he is conversant with the theory and practice of surveying, and is "devoted to it." He expresses his confidence in such a vocation, as opening a field to any one who will follow it industriously. In a subsequent letter these views are reiterated, with the further suggestion that he may not find the opportunity he seeks among the great cotton estates where he is,—for to do that, capital is needed,—but he looks to newer countries, such as Texas, or Kansas, or Arizona, where "*a man's a man for a' that.*" Not that he feels the return which he makes to be less than he receives; but, as he writes, "The whole of it is, I want to earn my living, which I am doing now, but in a very indefinite way."

And yet these earnest wishes are carefully subordinated to the judgment of his parent; so that when he receives the unexpected summons to turn his steps homeward, in order that all the details of a question so important to himself may be fully understood and properly determined, he responds at once, "As you know what is best for me, dear father, I will cheerfully and willingly follow your advice."

Accordingly, early in April, 1860, he finds himself once more amid the well-known scenes of his boyhood,—the happy little home that recalls so much, and the busy school, and so many comrades.

Upon full conversation and comprehension of Ulric's views and capabilities, his father consents to his return for the present; and by the middle of May he is once more on the banks of the Mississippi, actively engaged as before. The summer wears on, and events are transpiring which did not enter into consideration when he left the North.

The contest for the Presidency seems to involve more than the ordinary course of an election: the preference of the free States is plainly for Mr. Lincoln, and for a policy manifestly opposed to slavery, or rather to its extension. The South is more than indignant, even at such an avowal, and denounces it fiercely, yet will not agree on a single name in opposition, but permits the nomination of two candidates, divides its vote, and thus allows the choice to go adversely, which it could have determined otherwise. As the period of the election drew near, the symptoms of trouble became more portentous, and Ulric was recalled to his home; for his father was unwilling that one so much loved should be separated from the hearth-stone of the family at such a crisis.

He obeyed the call with his usual alacrity, took leave of his Southern friends, and returned to Washington in the latter part of September, 1860.

The moment seemed opportune for pursuing the

contemplated study of the law; and on the 22d of September he went to Philadelphia, to enter the office of his uncle, Mr. Jas. W. Paul, a prominent and highly-respected lawyer of that city.

To this new vocation Ulric applied himself with his habitual earnestness and diligence.

And thus the destiny of the youth reverted to the association where it truly belonged. It was a sore struggle to forsake a mode of life so well suited to his instincts,—the free, fresh air of the forest for the confined atmosphere of a large city, the wild excitement of the chase for the quiet avocation of the office, the untrammeled freedom of rural life for the guarded conventionalities of polite society.

And yet this active and fearless spirit cheerfully gave up his chosen pursuits, like a dutiful son, as he was, and set about his new calling with all the earnestness of an exalted nature.

It was hard to believe that the bold woodsman, who had so lately roved over hill and plain, forest and river, should be transformed so quickly into the quiet lad who now so tranquilly threaded the thronged streets, or bent him so intently over the desk. The hand, so used to the rifle and rein, was now given to the lighter task of pressing carefully the black-lettered page, and the eye that had beamed with delight at Nature in her wildest magnificence, now rested in calm contemplation of the mysteries of digests and commentaries. Throb on, brave young heart, in peace while you may, soon shall you be awakened to the thrilling sounds of battle, and be inspired by the holiest sentiments of our nature. *Then*, be hushed forever!

The remainder of 1860 was given to the business of the office, followed, after hours, by exercise at the gymnasium, and in the evening, by attendance at the Franklin Institute, for which he had great admiration. His time, as he writes, being divided thus: up at seven (November); at the office from eight to one; dinner, one to two; again at the office from two to half-past four P.M.; the gymnasium until six, then supper, ending with the Institute, where he remained until bedtime, at nine or ten o'clock.

Occasionally he speaks of friends whom he visits, particularly Captain Percival Drayton (of the navy), his father's well-tried and old comrade. He also meets his elder brother, Charles, who is engaged in steam engineering, and happens to be at Wilmington in the course of business.

At times, his letters report progress in the law, and satisfactory results of examinations.

But at no time is his attention diverted from the various phases of the great issues that are looming up about him like mighty shadows, threatening to involve in gloom the fairest future ever promised to a nation. The meeting of Congress is at hand, when the already well-known decision of the people will be formally announced. He writes, "I hope that pleasant relations will soon be restored between the North and South." Soon after, he mentions a grand Union meeting, which he hopes will serve as the initiative in restoring peace; looks on the present state of affairs as deplorable, etc.

And in his Christmas greeting, says, "I have been waiting anxiously to see something done by some party, and at last it has come in the shape of Fort Moultrie being abandoned, which will, no doubt, precipitate Southern action."

The considerate and temperate views of this mere lad were only those of the North, even at this time, when one star had shot madly from its place in the constitutional firmament, and had thus begun the work of dissolution, to which its policy for years had been pledged.

The public mind was deeply impressed with the nature of the crisis, but by no means to the extent competent to avert the evil; and the uncertainty as to the proper remedy which pervaded the masses who sustained the Union, confused opinion: President Buchanan openly announced that he had no power to *coerce*, and no right, if he had the power.

Whilst so many older and more experienced men hesitated, Ulric writes, about New Year's (1861), "I hope they will take some definite action." And a few days later, "Everything seems worked up to the highest pitch of excitement on account of political affairs generally." Still, his resolute, pleasant nature is not disturbed, nor driven to the advocacy of violent measures.

Before the first month of the new year ends, five States have withdrawn from the Union, and the last Southern man in the Cabinet has resigned. Ulric briefly remarks, "I would like much to belong to a military company;" for he fails not to notice some feeble move towards armament, and remarks on the quality of some military supplies that passed through the city to Fort Delaware.

During February he is still occupied with the law by day, and studies geology in the evening, not forgetting mathematics; anxiously concerned, however, about the pending troubles,—the rebellion having taken shape by the election of Mr. Jeff. Davis as its leader.

Military and naval officers, too, are resigning to follow their States.

About this time his brief letters, when referring to the state of affairs at Charleston, contain such remarks as, "The American flag should never have been insulted; there was no necessity for it. Anderson is a Southern man, yet he remains true to his duty, both to God and man."

CHAPTER II.

THE REBELLION.

AT this crisis Mr. Lincoln succeeded to the Presidency of the Union.

It may be said truly that history does not record an instance where a greater responsibility was devolved upon one man. The whole Southern section of the country had revolted from its sworn allegiance, and organized an independent government, that received from the State governments upon which it was based all that was needed to insure stability, as well as the capacity for instant and regular action in its operations. It was not the sudden and unprepared act of the moment, but had been previously concerted by the ablest leaders of the South, many of them with the advantage of official position in the Cabinet and Congress, as well as in the army and navy. Nor was the movement limited to measures merely civil; for secession was followed promptly by the seizure of the United States forts, navy-yards, arsenals, treasure, etc., while most of the Southern officers belonging to the seceding States joined the latter as rapidly as possible.

All this occurred before President Lincoln took the chair; so that, at the first moment of his accession, he found himself confronted by a powerful rebellion, ready, in every respect, to make good its defiance of the lawful government.

The free States, unprepared for this sudden and violent outrage, had not even agreed upon the remedy which the constitutional compact permitted in such a case. Opinions differed almost to opposition. While the great middle States that bordered on the South did not attempt to disguise their intention of joining the rebellion if the United States government ventured to coerce the seceding States, yet they barely abstained from action during the time that their senators and representatives retained their seats in Congress, and contributed to paralyze any measures which that body might be disposed to adopt to meet the emergency.

In truth, the loyal States had not reached the conclusion that force was expedient even if lawful. President Buchanan had openly declared against the doctrine of coercion; and, although the course of the South outraged the good sense and good feeling of Northern patriots, yet they hesitated to plunge the country into a civil war, which no human judgment could appreciate in duration or consequences.

To President Lincoln belonged the solution of this great problem. With all the sound sense and kindly feeling that so eminently distinguished this lamented statesman, he entered earnestly upon the appointed task, favoring any peaceful resort, but firmly maintaining the rights of the Constitution, while he abstained from all military measures that could aggravate the pending difficulties. Under his sagacious guidance peace and unity might have been restored to the land once more without bloodshed. But the desperate leaders of the slave power divined the probability of such a result, and hastened to avoid it by one fatal blow that should precipitate the impending struggle. Sumter was attacked, and its little garrison compelled to surrender to the forces of South Carolina.

The President immediately issued his proclamation for troops to regain possession of the United States property that had been seized by the insurgents from the first. The loyal States hesitated no longer, but wheeled promptly into line and responded to the call. The first levies were, however, necessarily directed to the preservation of the capital, which was now subjected to imminent peril by the sudden secession of the border States, and was actually brought into contact with Virginia, the most powerful of them. From this State, Washington was only separated by the Potomac, and was even controlled by the range of heights on its southern bank.

Disaffection had also been strongly manifested

in Maryland upon the first attempt to forward troops to Washington by the ordinary railroad route through that State. They were assailed by a mob in Baltimore, and only a single regiment, besides a few detached companies, succeeded in passing through the city.

The situation of the national government was thus rendered very precarious. With a mere handful of troops, not exceeding two thousand men, confronted by Virginia, cut off from the loyal States by Maryland, no communication open to reinforcements save by the Potomac,—a long and winding river flowing through insurrectionary territory, and therefore liable to obstruction,—it became a question whether the disloyal States should be first to the capture of Washington, or the loyal States to the rescue.

If the government of the United States had failed in the first instance to use its lawful power in checking the march of the rebellion at the outset, the latter proved to be quite as incapable of realizing the full advantage of its own prompt decision. With that preparation which a foreknowledge of its purpose permitted, it would have been easy to seize the capital by striking a rapid blow. As a consequence of such a step, Maryland would have been released from the Northern grip,—no small military gain, for the resolves of Mr. Davis and his coadjutors would have been very differently estimated by foreign powers if they had been issued from the halls which law and custom had consecrated to national legislation. It might even have been reasonably expected that the intense and ill concealed desire of England and France for the division of the great and growing power of the United States would, in such a case, have been fully expressed by an open recognition of the seceding States,—consequences which, collectively, the firmest believer in the power of the legitimate government might well hesitate to add to existing difficulties.

Amid this rush of events, which thus gathered about the capital, Ulric beheld his father involved. For quickly, upon the secession of the border States, the officers of the Washington Navy Yard, who happened to belong to them, abandoned their duty, to join the standards of what they considered their paramount allegiance; and the command of this most important position thereby devolved upon Captain Dahlgren, who alone remained faithful to his trust. He was aided by the gallant Wainwright, who afterwards fell a victim to the malaria of the Mississippi. The Navy Yard was not only valuable on account of the large quantities of cannon and ammunition which it contained, but it was also the key of our defenses on the left, controlling the bridge and the approaches by water from the eastern shore, and overawing the disaffected in that vicinity.

Whilst these and other incidents of the great drama were hastening into action, the youth looked on with as much calmness as the interest they inspired would permit. Unable at last to control his impulse, he seized the first opportunity that presented of being with his father, and left Philadelphia for Washington, on the 6th May, with his uncle, Mr. Abbott Lawrence. Along the whole route his observant eye encountered troops and trains. Arriving at the capital next day, he rambled over the Navy Yard, alive with the array of war and preparation. Passing into the city, he mingled with the crowd, gazed admiringly on the regiments arriving hourly, on the strong garrisons in the public buildings, and accompanied his uncle when he called on Major Anderson, fresh from Sumter. On Wednesday he walked over the Georgetown Heights, then the southern limit of the Union lines, and next day was at the Navy Yard near his father when he received President Lincoln. He was present at the various hospitalities extended to the chief magistrate,—at the concert and the review of that fine regiment, the New York 71st, then forming part of the garrison of the yard; and he witnessed the practice with the heavy navy cannon and howitzers, etc. In the evening Ulric was one of the throng that filled the rooms of the White House during the levee.

Next day (11th May) he returned to Philadelphia,

in order to remove thither his young brother and sister.

Meanwhile the preparation for enforcing the national authority, and for resistance, was proceeding actively. By the latter part of May the new levies had arrived in sufficient numbers to warrant measures for occupying the high ground near the capital, which constitutes its best natural defense to the southward; and, accordingly, a colunm was advanced from the city before daylight of the 24th of May, crossing the Long Bridge into Virginia; and thus, for the first time in our history, the troops of the Federal government entered upon armed occupation of the territory of a sovereign State in actual rebellion. At the same time a regiment of Zouaves, commanded by Colonel Ellsworth, and forming the left wing, was transported by water, in two Navy Yard steamers. Captain Dahlgren, as commandant of the yard, superintended this move in person, which was also covered at Alexandria by the guns of the Pawnee. The rebel troops, entirely unable to cope with this force, abandoned the town after a few musket-shots, and the Union colors were again hoisted in place of the flag that the insurgents had too long flaunted in sight of the capital. That cost the life of the gallant Colonel Ellsworth, who fell just after the event by the hand of an assassin. His body was borne back to the Navy Yard by Captain Dahlgren, on board the same steamboat on which he had but a few hours before conveyed this young officer to his last service.

A company of Virginia cavalry, under Captain Ball, became prisoners, and were transferred to the Navy Yard, where they were treated by Captain Dahlgren with a kindness that was acknowledged at the time, but not reciprocated at a later and a sadder day.

By this move General Scott secured the range of heights which commanded the capital in one direction, and all approaches to it from the other; together with the communication by water from our left to the city of Alexandria.

The month of June was spent in mutual preparation for decisive conflict. Regiments from loyal States accumulated rapidly in Washington, which, as they arrived, were advanced to the lines in front that the engineers were now establishing along the heights recently occupied. A considerable part of the force was conveyed by water, in the steamboats of the Navy Yard, directed by Captain Dahlgren; but the main body passed over the Long Bridge. About the middle of the month the rebels were obliged to evacuate Harper's Ferry, by reason of one of our columns advancing in that direction.

The North beheld with full confidence these measures for vindicating the supremacy of the

Union, and little doubt appeared to exist of their sufficiency to crush out the insurrection. Never before had a military array so imposing been collected under the national flag as that whose tents now whitened the hills of the Potomac; and perhaps such material as that composing it had never before gathered under any banner.

Desirous of gratifying the intense yearning of his son to look on such a spectacle, his father gave him leave to return home for awhile; and on the first day of July Ulric reached Washington. To him it seemed like a vast camp. Every train was freighted with new regiments, which found temporary abode in the public buildings or were transferred to the camp near the lines. The avenues were thronged with columns of infantry and artillery, gayly moving to the crash of numerous bands, while the townspeople looked on in wonder. The Navy Yard, too, was alive with preparation,—steamers arriving and departing freighted with troops and stores. Ordnance and ammunition were being accumulated and dispatched, whilst all the buildings that could be spared were occupied by a strong garrison, chiefly composed of the New York 71st. Their drills and those of the Naval Howitzer Companies, under Captain Parker, drew the attention of the crowds who daily visited the Yard.

The effect of such scenes upon the earnest nature

of the lad may well be imagined. He interested himself in all the proceedings, and everywhere had a hearty welcome from old friends or new.

By the middle of July the force about the capital had been swelled, by steady accessions, to an extent which seemed capable of meeting the general desire that one decisive blow should be struck, and it was generally understood that the hour of trial was at hand.

Those in insurrection had not been idle, however, and their determination to resist was as little understood as their ability to do so. It required an experience of four years to demonstrate both.

On the 16th July our army, about fifty thousand strong, was in motion; and on the 18th a collision occurred between its advanced detachments and some works held by the rebels, which our men assaulted, but were repulsed.

The 21st July, 1861, will ever be memorable as initiating the armed struggle which was to be prolonged until the section in rebellion was entirely exhausted.

The rebel army now held a well-chosen position at Manassas Junction, naturally of great strength, and that improved by careful engineering,—its advance resting on a small stream in the front, which gave its name to the battle.

Upon this the new levies of the republic were

launched under circumstances that would have tried older troops. The ground, broken by ravine and entangled by forest, permitted but a partial development of the whole force, a large portion of which was exhausted by marching and by want of food, a deprivation to which, as yet, the men were not accustomed. Still, most of the regiments which were actually engaged showed the best disposition, and, for awhile, the rebels were pressed so hard that, but for the timely arrival of Johnston on our right flank, the result might have been doubtful. This reinforcement, however, turned the scale, and produced so much confusion among our men that the retreat soon became a rout. Many of the brigades were entirely disorganized; cannon, ammunition, and baggage were abandoned by the way, and a large body of fugitives carried alarm to the capital itself, filling the streets with a panic-stricken and disorderly crowd. The whole army finally fell back until it rested on the Alexandria lines. The city seemed to be in imminent peril, more so, indeed, than it really was; for if the rebel leaders had followed up their success they would have experienced the difference between attacking and defending intrenched positions, especially with new troops. But they wisely forbore from a measure which would have stripped their victory of half its value; for, though our works were incomplete, and our men dispirited by the late reverse, they would have been found fully competent to retort severely if assaulted by the rebels.

The news of the disaster soon reached the Navy Yard. The commandant knew that the battle was going on, but the tidings which were received from time to time were favorable. Late in the afternoon the President drove down, and, to that hour, no adverse accounts had arrived. But it was hardly sunset when a telegram from the War Department to Captain Dahlgren requested the presence of "*an armed vessel at Alexandria to command as much as possible the approaches there*," which was met by sending the Perry, the only vessel of force at the Yard. This was sufficiently significant of a reverse, and the apprehension thus created was confirmed about an hour later by word that our army had been defeated and was in retreat.

On the following day and the succeeding, various requisitions were made on the Navy Yard for assistance and supplies, which were readily met by the commandant; and on the 24th he replied to a telegram from the Navy Department, by dispatching to the lines three heavy cannon (nine-inch) and five howitzers, with a prime body of trained seamen, under Captain Parker and other navy officers.

With this detachment went Ulric Dahlgren as aide to the commanding officer. And thus began that career in the service of his country which, for a short season only, was to be distinguished by the most unselfish devotion, by deeds of daring, by battle, by loss of limb, and, lastly, loss of life. He had shared deeply in the feelings of humiliation that pervaded the community at the recent defeat, unmixed with any lack of confidence in the ability of our soldiers to retrieve the disaster; and, with the permission of his father, he now joined the naval detachment about to be sent to the front.

The range of hills upon which were to be based the defenses of Washington to the southwest, includes the space formed by the bend of the Potomac at the Long Bridge, and sweeps from Alexandria in a curved line to the river above Georgetown. At this time the system of works was incomplete; and the demoralization consequent on the late check rendered it important that the defects should be looked to at once. The ridge did not extend entirely to Alexandria, but terminated a short distance from its outskirts, leaving an interval of low ground between its extremity and the river, by which a force might pass, seize the town, and turn the whole position on the heights by marching along its rear. Fort Ellsworth guarded the extreme left of the ridge, but could not check such a flank move, and would itself first be taken in reverse. To close this gap, the navy guns, under Lieutenant Parker, were posted on the brow of the crest looking towards the river, and so swept not only the approach but the passage, and effectually guarded the position from being taken in reverse.

It was half-past two P.M. on the 24th July, when the whole detachment left the Navy Yard, each nine-inch gun slung under a pair of wheels, drawn by a yoke of oxen. In about half an hour the party landed at Alexandria, and the heavy guns were put in motion at once, while the seamen drew the howitzers; the whole carefully equipped with tents, provisions, ammunition, etc. The subsequent events are thus briefly told by Ulric himself, in the official diary forwarded by Lieutenant Parker to Captain Dahlgren:

"NAVAL EXPEDITION FROM THE WASHINGTON NAVY YARD TO ASSIST IN THE DEFENSE OF ALEXANDRIA, VIRGINIA.

Lieutenant Commanding, F. A. PARKER;
Lieutenant, W. N. ALLEN; Master, D. C. WOOD;
Assistant Surgeon, A. B. JUDSON; Marine Officer, Lieut. CARTER;
Mr. ULRIC DAHLGREN.

"*Wednesday, July* 24, 1861.—Left the Navy Yard at half-past two P.M., with three nine-inch guns, four smooth twelve-pound howitzers, one rifled howitzer, and seventy seamen. Three P.M., landed at Alexandria, and proceeded to Fort Ellsworth, to remain there until a position for the battery could be determined by the engineer officer. Two nine-inch guns, and all the howitzers, ammunition, etc., were in the fort by midnight (the other gun would have been in also, but for an accident to the wheels by which it was slung); the men were assigned their places at the howitzers, and everything prepared to resist an attack. Lieutenant McCrea, with twenty seamen from the Pawnee, reported for duty; also Lieutenant Miller, with twenty seamen from the brig Perry. In the streets of Alexandria, and on the road to Fort Ellsworth, the volunteer soldiery were met in disorganized masses.

"*Thursday, July* 25.—The remaining nine-inch gun was brought into the fort at eight A.M. The position for the battery was determined by Colonel Franklin at eleven A.M. Two platforms were finished and the breastworks commenced by dark. The men and carpenters at work until midnight, after which all hands returned to Fort Ellsworth. *Midnight.*—Davenport, of the brig Perry, relieved Lieutenant Miller. Commandant Dahlgren visited the battery, accompanied by Colonel Franklin and Captain Rowan of the Pawnee. Great disorganization observed among the volunteers in the neighboring camps.

"*Friday, July* 26.—Tents pitched and guns mounted by night. Eight more men from the brig Perry reported. Soldiers visited the camp in large numbers during the day; they expressed great surprise at the rapidity with which the guns were mounted and prepared for action, and also a determination to stand by the 'boys' to the last. Hoisted our flag amid the cheers of the men, and gave the name of 'Fort Dahlgren' to the work.

"*Saturday, July* 27.—Shell-pit dug out and magazine finished. Marines increased to forty men and a lieutenant. The volunteers seem to be reorganizing.

"*Sunday, July* 28.—No work done. Men and arms inspected. General McClellan and General McDowell, with staff, visited the battery in the afternoon; also Captain Rowan of the Pawnee, accompanied by several other officers of the navy.

"*Monday, July* 29.—Shell-pit covered, and the men working in the trenches. Commandant Dahlgren visited the battery; also Senator Rice (Minnesota).

"*Tuesday, July* 30.—All hands working in trenches. Lieutenant McCrea detached, together with Pawnee's men. Men at quarters in the evening. Various volunteer regiments drilling; their condition seems greatly improved.

"*Wednesday, July* 31.—Men working in trenches. Rest after dinner; at quarters, and a howitzer drill in the evening. Volunteers drilling also.

"*Thursday, Aug.* 1.—Men unable to work, on account of rain. At quarters, and drill at the heavy guns in the evening. Dress-parade of volunteers in the neighboring camps during the afternoon.

"*Friday, Aug.* 2.—Men working in the trenches. Flag of truce arrived near here. Men ordered to Fort Ellsworth to witness an execution. At quarters in the evening, and a drill at the heavy guns. Dress-parade of volunteers in the neighboring camps.

"*Saturday, Aug.* 3.—Men working in the trenches this morning. Exercise at great guns and howitzer battery. Lieutenant Carter (marines) detached, and Lieutenant Huntingdon reported for duty.

"(Signed) FOXHALL A. PARKER,
"*Lieut. U. S. Navy.*"

The perfect order with which the whole operation was conducted, the celerity of movement, the completeness of equipment, the discipline and thorough training of the seamen, under such good officers, was a lesson to the young beginner which answered as well as a longer schooling would have done in a less urgent state of things; of this he reaped the full benefit.

General McClellan arrived on the 27th July, and took command of the Army of the Potomac. Confidence and a better feeling returned with order; and as new levies began to come in, the desire to move onward revived. It was assented to, however, on all sides, that in order to do this we needed a larger force than had been contemplated before, as well as a higher condition of discipline.

The rebels, finding that the Union forces adhered to the lines of the capital, occupied with detachments the ground thus left vacant in front, and closed their skirmishers to the Union positions, particularly at Munson's Hill, an eminence contiguous to our advanced posts.

It required but a few days for the experienced officer in command of the naval battery to get it into perfect condition; the platforms were laid, the cannon mounted, the magazines for powder and shell provided, the men properly camped, fed, and drilled, sentries posted, etc., and then nothing remained but to await whatever demand might arise for real service. This period of inaction was used by Ulric in exploring the neighboring camps, and gathering instruction from the continual process of organization by which the armed multitude was to be converted into a military body. For the public were now convinced that more was needed than numbers to do the work required; in which conviction our men concurred fully, and, with hearty good will, submitted to all the severity and exactness of routine which the occasion demanded. Ulric saw daily brigades and divisions being created and wrought, by drill and discipline, into effective shape, and witnessed the accumulation of war material in such quantities and excellency as perhaps no other army had ever been so well equipped with.

In thus passing time, he often encountered many who had served in the navy and were friends of his father; for this mighty host had been volunteered from the nation without regard to classes or previous vocation, and the military movement by water was not unfrequently accelerated by the handicraft of the sailor-soldiers in its ranks. One of the regiments was commanded by an officer (Colonel McC. Murphy) who had served in the same ship with Captain Dahlgren. The lad also made friends for himself, and before long he was led by this association among the skirmish lines thrown out to feel and annoy the rebel outposts. One of these outposts was Munson's Hill, a prominent elevation, where floated a rebel standard that was seen distinctly from the Navy Yard, and where the practice of good marksmen made adventure quite as dangerous as interesting. Here the young aide might often be seen, with his keen eye glancing over the sights of a delicate and beautiful Maynard rifle. He writes on the 5th September:

"I am in the midst of very exciting and interesting events. Last Friday and Saturday I was in two skirmishes near Munson's Hill, in which we lost several killed and wounded, and they lost some also. It is regular Indian-fighting that we do every day near here, and I have a Maynard rifle, with which *I send a telegram* south occasionally. At present, my knees are so sore from crawling in the bushes, and fighting them in their own style, that I can hardly walk."

For this life in camp and of adventure much of previous habits and training fitted him admirably. Though very slim and light in flesh, he was capable of any endurance, and still delighted in the pursuits which had their place in the open air.

Occasionally he visited his father, at the Navy Yard, and witnessed passing events there. Sometimes the presence of a foreigner of distinction lent an interest to the occasion, and testified the friendly feelings felt in our progress. Among these, no one was more prominent than the excellent Prince de Joinville, who never failed to evince his solicitude for the re-establishment of the Union, and at last shared in the perils of the battle-field. With him were his two nephews, the Count of Paris and the Duke de Chartres, both of whom wore the Union uniform as captains on the staff of the general.

Prince Napoleon also visited the Navy Yard early in August, and, to his honor, was known to have entertained and expressed friendly sentiments to the Union cause, though such were by no means fashionable at the Imperial Court.

By the middle of September it became evident that it would be impossible to organize so large an army for active operations before the advent of the winter; therefore no movement of any consequence could be anticipated before the spring. To this delay even the general impatience was forced to submit.

Ulric was therefore dispatched to Philadelphia in order to resume his studies during this period of inaction. The remarkable facility with which he yielded his own wishes to those of his father was never more strikingly exemplified than in this instance. Putting aside his rifle, and all the "pride, pomp, and circumstance of glorious war," he departed for Philadelphia, and again took his place at the desk, as cheerfully as if his earnest nature had never been absorbed in the great events of the passing struggle, nor burned with intense desire to bear any part, however humble, in the cause of his country.

He was assured, however, that when the appointed hour of action should come, he would be recalled to share in the first opportunity for service that might offer; and he felt consoled in that knowledge.

The study of the law was varied, as before, by exercise and by a quiet evening with some friend. Other objects also presented themselves to his attention. It was at this time that his father gave him the copyright of a formula for the drill of his own eleven-inch gun, and Ulric had it printed and published as afterwards circulated in the navy by the order of the Bureau of Ordnance.

A number of patriotic young gentlemen of the city also associated to form a light-artillery company; and Ulric, as one of the members, entered with his wonted zeal and activity into the practical execution of the project. His letters to his father interested the latter, so that four navy howitzers were loaned to the company for its use. In one letter he narrates an interview, in relation to this purpose, with the commandant of the Navy Yard (Philadelphia), Commodore Pendergrast, who had commanded the Merrimac when Ulric was on board, some years past, during the trip to Annapolis. The gallant veteran had not forgotten his young guest, and taking him aside, after business with the captain of the howitzer company, he doffed his official bearing, and indulged in a hearty laugh with the lad.

Among the events of the day, he does not forget the navy, but exults in the capture of Port Royal by Admiral Dupont, and remarks, "*The war-ships showed their teeth, and how deep they could bite.*"

The period was at hand when the scene was to open on the soldier-life of the young patriot, and when, freed from every trammel, he was to take the part he so well sustained under many trials,—never ceasing from that solemn duty until death released him forever.

CHAPTER III.

HARPER'S FERRY.

THE Union had at last an army in the field that seemed capable of realizing every wish of the country. It was numerous, well appointed, and as well trained as the efforts of able officers, unceasingly exerted for nine months, could make it. At its head was a leader in whom the troops and the President had full confidence.

The spring was advancing, and the miry roads of Virginia were beginning to harden sufficiently for the movements of the army and its heavy trains.

The whole nation was expectant, for our great host was about to move, and we were evidently at the threshold of important events. The ardent nature of the young student was stirred to its inmost depths. He could brook inactivity no longer, nor fix his thoughts on the quiet pursuits of the law-office when the din of arms resounded throughout the land, and every loyal heart was bent on the coming struggle, which again it was fondly hoped would crush the rebellion at a blow.

In his gentle but earnest manner, Ulric made known his wishes to his father, who yielded to them without hesitation.

And so, not hastily, but carefully, and almost reverentially, the youth laid down the reasonings of the great expounders of the law, that he might take his place in the ranks; for he felt that the argument had been closed forever in the great council of the nation, and that the decision lay with the sword.

The thoroughness with which he fulfilled every duty or purpose was never more strikingly exemplified than in the closely-written memoranda of his legal studies. The lectures of Judge Sharswood, which he attended at the law school, are faithfully minuted to the last, in a clear, regular hand, without a single blemish. The last is, "*Examination, Feb.* 24, 1862."

It was about the middle of April that he repaired to Washington, and took his place near his father to assist in the labors of the naval ordnance, for which his previous training so admirably qualified him. In former days it had been a pastime, now it was to be a duty as well as a pleasure; and in the discharge of that duty he felt himself to be no privileged incumbent. With the quiet, unassuming manner that always marked his deportment, he was to be seen, early and late, industriously occupied with such writing, or drafting, or other duty, as might be assigned him.

It was this never-failing integrity of purpose that won him the perfect confidence of his father; for it was not a mere habit,—it was part and parcel of his nature; he could not do otherwise.

Ulric had now just completed his first score of years. The healthy hue previously acquired in the playground of the schoolboy, and deepened almost to bronzing by Western life, was lost in the seclusion of a student; and he had also run up to a stature of six feet, too rapidly for the close knitting of his frame.

Still, he was active, well practiced in the training of the gymnasium, capable of any fatigue, in perfect health, and fully endowed with that elasticity of mind and body which youth and health alone can confer.

The hours that remained from the labors of his office were mostly passed in the stately but quaint old mansion which his father inhabited as commandant of the Navy Yard. There Hull and other well-known sea-commanders had lived, and some had died;* and in its long galleries, late in the day, young Ulric might be seen, seated in thoughtful repose near the door, his eye wandering over the singularly contrasted view of green trees and shrubbery, from which rose here and there the tall chim-

* The author of this memoir, Admiral Dahlgren, died at this residence, July 12, 1870.

neys of busy forges and glowing furnaces. Or in the quiet dining-room, father and son might be found over the daily meal, in happy companionship.

And thus passed the hours and the days of the young man,—brightly, joyously, with duty before him; yet he was not unobservant of passing events, and was only biding his time.

On special occasions he had opportunities of seeing some of the great actors in the national drama, and of being near them. In one instance he was invited aboard the Miami, when the President went down the Potomac, with his Secretaries of War and Treasury, to have personal cognizance of affairs at Acquia, which had just then been occupied by our forces under General McDowell, who came on board the Miami to pay his respects to the President as soon as he heard of his arrival. Ulric listened with no little zest to the recital of the operation from the commanding officer, and to what he had to say of Bayard's cavalry exploits; and he saw the name of that gallant officer penciled down by the Secretary of War for promotion to the rank of brigadier-general, little thinking in his freest fancy that the same hand would sign his commission as colonel in scarcely more than a year, when he would be told that intermediate grades had been passed over because of his distinguished service.

Even so, brave boy, and before the year is

ended, the hills you now look on will behold you spurring fresh from daring deeds at Fredericksburg.

Events now come hastening thickly on. McClellan is in Yorktown, has pushed by Williamsburg, and is approaching Richmond with the eagles of the republic. McDowell's force has been swelled by additions to a goodly army, and he is soon to advance and join McClellan.

The President wishes to look on this array before it departs on its appointed task. So, with the Secretary of War, he descends the Potomac, traverses the short rail-track from Acquia, and is gladly welcomed by the generals and their battalions.

It is one of the bright days of latter May, when he enters a spacious old Virginia mansion built on a terraced hill, looking down upon the rushing Rappahannock, and almost into the streets of the ancient city of Fredericksburg on the opposite shore, — its ample halls and fair gardens very suggestive of a former state of things, but now abandoned by its misguided owner to the tread of strangers.

Presently the streets resound to the tramp of chargers bearing the chief of the republic, and the generals and officers of all grades who surround him. He surveys the massive columns of brave men, who move by with measured tread to the strains of martial music. The pageant is over, the President departs, the soldier returns to his tent, and the old town to its slumbers, not to be disturbed again by the unlooked-for apparition of Union troops until young Ulric charges through its avenues, saber in hand, and scatters its chivalry like sea-drift before the gale. But before that hour shall come, the glorious boy shall witness other sights, and shall see the tide of war recoil to the very portals of our capital, after treading many a battle-field himself.

On Saturday, the 24th of May, long before daylight, Captain Dahlgren's steamer, bearing the President, reached the Navy Yard at Washington. Just as he was stepping ashore, a messenger handed him a telegraphic dispatch. No one near surmised its importance. The President passed to the carriage in waiting, and was driven off.

The information was startling: the rebels, eluding Frémont, had suddenly concentrated a strong force upon General Banks's little column, severed his communications, and were moving towards Harper's Ferry.

We know now that the object was to divert the army of McDowell from joining that of McClellan, and that the rebels had learned the exposed condition of Harper's Ferry, and the lack of concentration along its approaches.

Banks was surprised, and barely able to effect the escape of his small force across the Potomac at Williamsport; while Jackson, foiled in this respect, turned his advance towards Harper's Ferry. The proposed object was speedily effected, and McDowell, who was to march south on the following Monday, received orders to move towards the valley, whilst Frémont converged towards the same quarter, in the hope of cutting off Jackson's retreat.

During these movements, the alarm at Harper's Ferry was increased to a panic, for the place was totally unprepared to meet the emergency. The War Department, however, sent forward strong reinforcements and abundant supplies. The Navy Department also contributed its aid, in the shape of some heavy cannon, and a battery of navy howitzers manned by a body of select seamen and in charge of two very young men: one was Acting Master Daniels; the other, *Ulric Dahlgren.*

The calm of a quiet Sabbath rested on the busy workshops of the Navy Yard; and it was only about its ordnance department that a few lingered to meet some pressing demands which would brook no delay. Unusual tranquillity reigned in the city, for the tide of war had been rolled far away, until it came in view of the spires of Richmond itself.

Ulric and his father had both left the Navy Yard, to spend the day peacefully at the sanctuary and at home.

Suddenly comes the brief query by telegraph to the commandant of the Yard,—"*Can you send any howitzers to Harper's Ferry?*" To which was returned the prompt reply,—"*Yes; and some heavy cannon.*" Forth goes the order, and, without the least delay, the artillery, large and small, with all their appliances, are dragged through the quaint old gateway, accompanied by a party—not large, but choice—of veteran seamen. Like the *Guard*, they are only summoned into active service upon great emergencies,—for their labors are needed in the work of preparation.

By the evening the whole detachment, cannon, howitzers, and ammunition, and men, young and old, are borne swiftly on the rail-cars towards Harper's Ferry, which they reach early on Monday morning, just as several regiments are arriving. General Saxton is in command.

The cannon and the seamen have the air of service, and as they pass along are cheered by parties of soldiers. But it will be no child's play to drag the ponderous nine-inch gun away up that mountain-side, so as to command the approaches far and near. Much hard toil will it need, and some wit, too; but it is done at last, and the labor is almost forgotten in the pride of seeing the huge pieces ready for action, and perched some two thousand feet* above the level of the sea.

Those rugged tars know what they can do, and how to do it; they have a pride, too, in that earnest, active lad, young Ulric, for they know him, he is one of them, and has almost grown up among them. That hearty veteran has taught him to swim,—another, to handle the oar,—and all have seen him over and over again looking at some passage in their daily toil, and as deeply interested as themselves in its success; now steering the cutter which their well-strung sinews are driving swiftly over the placid stream, or intently watching them handling the heavy cannon, or the light howitzer, his steady nerves unstartled by the crashing din that jars all around as the shot issues forth in living flame. Nor is his own hand wanting where it can serve. There is not a gun, old or new, smooth or rifled, that he has not seen tried in every quality, and

---

* "U. S. Military Telegraph, from Harper's Ferry,
11 A.M. May 27, 1862.

"To CAPTAIN DAHLGREN.

"SIR,—I have arrived and reported in obedience to orders. The nine-inch gun is stationed on the heights opposite Harper's Ferry, and over two thousand feet above the level of the sea. The howitzer battery has not, as yet, been assigned to any place, but expect it to move with the army.

"Very respectfully,
"C. H. DANIELS,
"*Commanding Naval Battery.*"

adjudged; and so, also, with shot, and shell, and fuses, in every variety that genius or caprice can conceive. This is the sailor's vocation, with which he is so familiar, while *they* are strangers to much that he is gleaning in silent study from black-lettered books, rich with the knowledge of others.

They know, too, that he is a brave boy, who never falters at anything, and yet no braggart, but modest and gentle as a girl; with never an unkind word for the humblest of them, but always their fast friend. Happily, they see not into the future, and therefore are unconscious that other duties to their young companion are to be rendered. They will carry him some day on his weary litter, wounded, from the battle-field, will look on his mutilated form, will give kind and gentle aid to the sufferer during the vigils of many a long night, and bear witness in their own hearts to the unvarying nobleness of his young nature. So the rough old seamen love the boy whom they have seen shoot up almost to manhood, and have that feeling for him which none but such as they can have for a young comrade.

And thus the little band, though suddenly brought together, contained all the elements of strength and ready assimilation. The naval battery did good work when called upon, and every man was proud of it, and knew that the general only did them justice when he recognized their labors in his official report.

For two days General Saxton was engaged feeling in every direction for the enemy, and his skirmishers did not go far without having assurance that the position was surrounded by a strong force, which peeped out only at times from the cover of the underwood. Occasionally the rebel skirmishers advanced, and then firing occurred.

Late on the 29th, Ulric Dahlgren was sent down to Washington to obtain additional supplies of ammunition. The evening was far advanced when he arrived, and found his father at the War Department, in the private office of the Secretary, where was also the President, occupied with the information arriving by telegraph from the armies. What the lad had to say was of interest, and was clearly narrated, both to the President and to Secretary Stanton.

As he was passing out, the latter, in his brief and emphatic manner, tendered Ulric an appointment as additional aide-de-camp, with the rank of captain. The unexpected favor was promptly received, with every mark of satisfaction and gratitude. Late as it was, the indefatigable Adjutant-General was still at his post in another part of the building; so the necessary documents were made out at once, and the delighted Ulric was duly sworn, and left the War Department with all the newly-acquired honors of a captain,—more valued, perhaps, at his age (just twenty), than those of any rank afterwards attained.

The next morning he was early on his way back, in the full uniform of his new position; which he had obtained at the no small discomfort of some unlucky tailor, whose hours of rest had been broken to meet the sudden demand of one who always went earnestly and promptly to his end, whatever it might be. He arrived just in time to take part in the final repulse of the rebels from Harper's Ferry.

General Saxton, anticipating an attempt to outflank him, had drawn in his force on Bolivar Heights, and concentrated it about the Maryland Heights, where his heavy guns were posted. The skirmishers on both sides were frequently engaged, and once the rebels came on so persistently that Saxton drew in even his pickets, so as to let his guns have fair sweep. Captain Ulric was out gathering in our skirmishers, when the rebels opened with shell, some of which burst quite near enough to him, but without disturbing his composure, which was too natural to need even the baptism of battle.

The day closed, and our weary men had lain down to rest near their arms, with little expectation of being disturbed; for the heavy storm which had been looming up was now abroad in its fury. The mountains were shaken by the crashing thunder, the sight was dazzled by the vivid lightning, and the very sluices of the heavens seemed opened. Regardless of the violence of the tempest, the rebels advanced to carry our position. Just at the right moment the navy nine-inch guns on the Maryland Heights opened fire, and their bursting shells announced our readiness for the attack. Little expecting such a warm reception from that quarter, the astonished rebels fell back, after an effort of an hour's duration.

About midnight, some Louisiana and Mississippi regiments were hurled at our lines, but in vain; and they quickly withdrew. The next morning it was found that the enemy had retreated by way of Charlestown. They were gone, indeed, but they had accomplished their main purpose; for they had compelled McDowell to abandon his advance towards Richmond and to turn off in their pursuit to Front Royal.

And so, suddenly and without warning, Ulric passed from civil life to the field, and rejoiced in all that belonged to his new calling. He was once more, as he loved to be, in the free air of heaven, his frame invigorated and his spirit buoyant with its freshness. Around him nature displayed her grandest scenery in wild sublimity. For here the river wound its way among the rocky bases of the great mountains that rose towering to the heavens, just as they appeared of old, from the first foundations of the earth; clad in the primeval forest, and seamed by ravines into whose deep shadows the light of day goes not; while from every peak and cliff the sunlight glitters in fullest blaze,—mountain after mountain crowding in every variety of tint and outline, until their distant blue nearly blends with that of the heavens.

Who can tell the rapture that filled the swelling heart of the noble youth as his steed bore him swiftly over the winding road, or toiled with sure foot up the steep ascent, whence the delighted eye wandered over every form of hill and dale? Well might he say, as he gazed, that "*beautiful*" *failed to convey the idea*,—that it was the "sublime" that held his soul enrapt.

General Saxton, having so creditably acquitted himself of the duty assigned him, took leave for another field, and handed over his charge to General Sigel. Captain Ulric, preferring to remain, found himself on the staff of the newly-arrived commander, who quickly put his forces in motion to follow the footsteps of the retreating rebels.

The thick clouds that had been gathering in the mountains broke at length into heavy rain, flooding the roads and swelling the rills into torrents.

But Sigel knew that no time was to be lost if pursuit was to be of any avail; and so, amid all the discomfort of deep mud and drenched garments, his columns pushed on; the young captain heeding as little as the hardiest the pelting storm and the scanty fare,—nights without sleep, or even a spot of dry earth on which to stretch his wearied limbs. He had often gone through more inconvenience for mere pastime, and what was it to his elastic sinews now that so noble and patriotic an object was in view? So he patiently marches on, content with the first friendly hearthstone where he may wring the moisture from his soaked clothing, and feel as light and as satisfied as if rain and wind had not touched him.

He is in his element, and *begins as he will end, ahead with his troopers,*—now searching Smithfield for a rebel flag, and then, with willing spirits ready for any adventure, in quest of some rebel officers. But pursuit has its termination as well as battle, and when Winchester is reached, Sigel's corps, reduced in number and in ill condition, must pause and act as a reserve.

For, on the 6th of June, Frémont, in trying to stop Jackson, has reached Harrisonburg, and on the 8th has overtaken his rear at Cross Keys, and handled it roughly; but the next day, Shields, anxious to have a hand in the fray, besets the retreating enemy with too little force, and suffers severely.

On the 12th, Frémont has got as far down the valley as Mount Jackson; but the rebel force is now out of reach; and so ends for the present the advance of our own divided columns. The march of the First Corps is arrested, therefore, at Winchester, where Sigel is to put it into good condition for the campaign.

Meanwhile his aide rides around the neighborhood, and explores every road and pass, which is soon done, and he is threatened with idle time. To avoid this, he bethinks him of the ordnance of the corps, and interests himself in finding out what it is and what it needs. The general, who is an artillerist, is not unwilling that the spare time of Captain Ulric should be given in this direction. The guns are soon put through an inspection, every detail is carefully examined, and then they are dragged out to try the ammunition, and the shells, and the fuses; a practice-ground is improvised, and the ranges are determined by an off-hand imitation of what the captain was so familiar with in his father's department. Next comes a lengthy and critical report, which is appreciated by the general.

On the 23d June the First Corps was marched to Middletown by way of Front Royal; and here Ulric writes his father that he thinks the horse which he has just bought for him, and which he admires very much, may prove too young to stand all his riding, which requires two or three horses; that it needs some training, too, which he proposes to enter upon at once, as he has pretty fully disposed of all his ordnance cares.

Ulric was a graceful and skillful rider, and had a

perfect passion for horses from his early childhood. If he had been given to many words, he might perhaps have said as much for the horse as did the emperor's esquire, Pughliano, in his stable, of whom Sir Philip Sidney writes (1573): "Then would he adde certaine praises, by telling what a peerless beast the horse was, the only serviceable courtier without flattery, the beast of most beauty, faithfulnesse, courage, and such more, that if I had not bin a peece of a logician before I came to him, I think he would have perswaded me to have wished myself a horse."

It was interesting to observe his wonderful tact in managing horses. There was none of the ostentatious parade of a jockey, but a quiet way of bringing himself in contact with the animal by passing his hand kindly and softly about the head and neck and shoulders, and carefully avoiding whatever was sensitive; so that the horse seemed to recognize the friendly touch, and the most restive found him mounted before there was a chance for rebelling.

Captain Ulric was not merely a graceful horseman, but could also withstand any amount of hard riding, and had wonderful endurance, as he proved on many occasions, such as his ride from Falmouth with orders to Sigel, then at Dumfries; a distance, by the road, of nearly twenty miles, which he accomplished in about two hours, and returned by five o'clock next morning, traveling more than fifty miles, after having been in the battle the preceding day.

In his last service to Richmond he was almost continuously in the saddle for three days and nights, showing less fatigue than most of those around him, though he had lost a leg and was still reduced in strength from the effects of the wound.

Captain Ulric was thus fitting himself for service at hand, while the forces of Frémont, Banks, and McDowell were consolidating into one army under General Pope, styled the *Army of Virginia*,—a very necessary measure, for the division of commands had worked badly, and was justly considered as chargeable with the ill success of the attempt to repel Jackson's raid through the valley.

June 29, he writes that he is still busy with artillery matters, adding, "We are between Middletown and Strasburg, and are looking for Jackson in every direction, but cannot find him." He concludes with the remark, "*There will soon be something heard from him, either here or at Richmond.*"

Well judged, young captain! At that very time he *was* heard from, and where it was least convenient,—on McClellan's right flank at Richmond.

During the month of July, the Army of Virginia was chiefly occupied in getting into good condition, though there were several small affairs between advanced parties on both sides,—at Culpepper, Gordonsville, Orange Court House, and North Anna. But all attention was drawn to the vicinity of Richmond, where the rebels had succeeded in forcing McClellan back on James River and were then employed in watching his movements.

On the 26th July, Sigel occupied Madison Court House, with the First Connecticut Cavalry. Once only during this month (on the 17th) was Ulric in Washington, and then in order to procure ammunition for the corps. He was now in fine health and spirits; for the life he led was well adapted to the development of both,—ever active, sleeping and eating wherever the night found him, and invigorated by the bracing mountain air.

CHAPTER IV.

CAMPAIGN WITH THE ARMY OF VIRGINIA, JULY TO NOVEMBER, 1862.

THE month of July, 1862, seemed to be a period of inaction with both parties; whereas it was, in fact, a season in which each was preparing for a decisive blow, and vigilantly observing the movements of the other, in order to regulate thereby his own. The rebels had the advantage of a united army on a single interior line, while the Union forces were divided into two armies, separated by a considerable distance,—not in communication, and not to be connected, except by a circuitous route involving delay and danger.

So long as McClellan actively menaced Richmond from the James River, Pope was undisturbed in the concentration and reorganization of the scattered columns in Northern Virginia. But as soon as McClellan seemed unable to advance, the rebels were felt by Pope to be in force in his front; and the withdrawal of the Union army from the James River was the signal for the rebels to move forward promptly and in full force upon Washington.

On the 29th of July, General Pope left Washington and arrived at Warrenton. A few days previously, Sigel had advanced the 1st Connecticut Cavalry to Madison Court House.

On the 3d of August, General McClellan was ordered to withdraw from the James River.

And on the 9th of August, Jackson again struck at Banks, on Cedar Mountain.

There had been some premonitions through the day of the coming blow, but the evening drew on without decided appearances, until about five o'clock, when the rebel infantry advanced in force. Our men resisted gallantly, being encouraged by the presence and example of their general (Banks), but were gradually forced back by superior numbers.

Sigel, with his corps (First), was at Sperryville on the evening of the 8th August (Friday), when an orderly rode in at full speed, with orders to march in an hour by way of Culpepper, as the rebel troops were approaching.

It was late, however, in the following evening before Sigel reached the ground, when his corps was pushed to the front, and that of Banks withdrawn, much weakened by its severe losses.

About this time, the enemy, finding that fresh troops were coming against him, drew off in the obscurity of the night. Captain Dahlgren had been able to precede the march of the wearied infantry of the corps by a few hours, and reached the scene of action, as he writes, "in time to go through the battle. During the night, a rebel battery having moved out against us, I asked permission to drive it away, which was most effectually done. General Sigel complimented me on the battle-field next morning."

In a subsequent letter, he makes more particular mention of this little incident, in the following words:

"The annexed sketch will show the nature of the country, and relative position of our batteries with theirs.

"The battle was fought near the mountain, the position of General Banks's corps being very nearly as marked on the sketch *a*, *a*, *a*, etc. About dark, they fell back behind the line of woods marked *b*, and still later, behind the ridge marked *c*, *c′*, leaving nothing between this ridge, which was occupied by our artillery, and the woods *b*. General Sigel's corps had come up and occupied the ground *d*, *d′*, General McDowell's being near that marked *e*, *e*. Captain Reynolds's battery was at *f*, and a New York battery at *g*.

"General Sigel, with his staff, rode down the road towards the woods *b*, and when within four or five hundred yards of it, a battery, which the rebels had advanced on the road through the woods, commenced firing from a small hill, marked *m*, at General McDowell's batteries *c′*, *c′*, which was

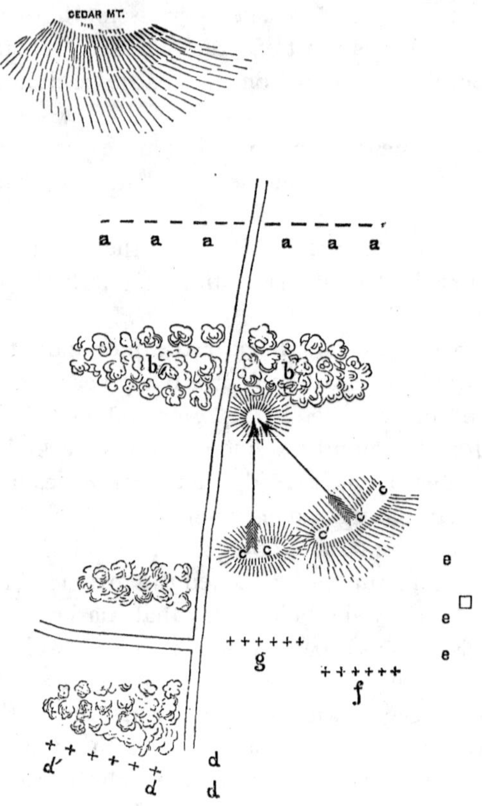
CEDAR MT.
a a a a a a
b b
c c c c c
d d d d d'
e e e
g
f

briskly replied to by them (the line of fire being represented by *m—c′*); I should judge the distance to have been about thirteen or fourteen hundred yards at least.

"I immediately asked permission to bring one of our batteries to the point *c*, where, at a distance of seven or eight hundred yards, we could enfilade the rebels. The request being granted, I could not find any of our batteries near enough, and therefore placed the battery *g* at *c*, and then sighted each gun myself, and gave the order to fire by section; which being done, the rebel battery ceased firing and retreated through the woods, leaving the captain, a lieutenant, and fourteen horses dead on the hill. On examination in the morning, all the shots were proved, by the wounds of men and horses, to have come from the direction *m—c*, and were those of rifled three-inch guns. Many twelve-pound shot and shell were found in the neighborhood; but all those persons who examined the spot agreed on this point: that the battery *g* did all the damage that was done, and forced the rebels to leave their position. Those who observed the relative position of the batteries came to the same conclusion.

On the 16th of August, the last of our men left James River; and Richmond being thus relieved of all fear, the rebel leaders lost no time in turning their entire army on Pope. He lay along the Rapidan, in position, about the 12th of August, with his left, under Reno, at Raccoon Ford; the center, under McDowell, occupying both flanks of Cedar Mountain; and Sigel's corps, as his extreme right, at Robertson's Run. Information from many sources began to reach him that Jackson was being largely reinforced from Richmond.

On the 16th, his cavalry captured Stuart's adjutant-general, with a letter on his person from General Lee, showing the force of the rebels, and the intention to overwhelm General Pope before the army of McClellan could reinforce him. On the 18th of August, Pope was satisfied by several indications that the entire rebel army was in front of him, and only separated by the river. He wisely judged his position too advanced for his inferior force, and decided to withdraw behind the Rappahannock with all possible speed; which was effected, without molestation, on the 18th and 19th,—Sigel crossing at Sulphur Springs. Our army now lay behind the Rappahannock, with Sigel on the right, about three miles above Rappahannock Station, and the left at Kelly's Ford.*

The enemy advanced to the river, and felt the several fords. During the whole of the 21st and 22d, there was an incessant blaze of artillery from both sides of the river along a distance of seven or eight miles; during which, vigorous efforts were

---

* Swinton, 176.

made by the enemy to cross. But they were as often driven back; and General Sigel even took the offensive at Freeman's Ford, and followed with the division of Schurz. The rebels concentrated in force, when an obstinate action ensued; and our men were finally pushed back, losing General Bohlen. On this occasion Captain Dahlgren was useful in assisting to cover the repassage of the river by our troops, under an annoying artillery fire. He so placed a battery, and cut a line through the woods for its fire, as to enfilade the guns of the enemy, and, opening from this unexpected quarter, compelled them to retire.

Finding it impossible to force the passage of the Rappahannock, the enemy left a portion of his army in our front, and moved the remainder up the river, intending to outflank our right. But this was prevented for the time by a corresponding move on the part of General Sigel, who advanced towards Sulphur Springs, and encountered the rebels about two miles from that place, at Great Run, driving them back over it. He then crossed the run, and occupied Sulphur Springs under a heavy fire of artillery. In the course of these operations, General Sigel put Captain Dahlgren in charge of a regiment of infantry and two guns, with directions to harass the enemy's left, and outflank it if possible. The young aide, after a hard and rapid march, succeeded in coming into contact with the enemy, whom he attacked, and silenced their battery; but the night coming on, they took advantage of it to retreat over the run. The movement had the desired effect, and was "executed to the full satisfaction of the general;"* who adds, "*Captain Dahlgren's services, generally, on the line of the Rappahannock, where he was continuously engaged in meeting the enemy's batteries with our own, to facilitate thereby the march of our troops and trains alongside of the river, were most valuable.*"

The enemy continued to manœuvre around our right, and gradually accomplished his purpose of outflanking in that direction. On the 25th, he reached Salem by a forced march of thirty-five miles, and next day passed through Thoroughfare Gap, reaching Bristow Station of the railroad by sunset.

The quick perception of the commander of the First Corps kept him fully alive to the design of the enemy, as his official report shows. On the 27th, the Union army was swinging round to meet the new position of the enemy, and battle was evidently becoming imminent.

But these seemingly interminable and fruitless efforts to intercept the enemy's advance were beginning to wear heavily on the moral and physical condition of our men. The commanding general

---

* General Sigel,—private letter.

states that from the 18th to the 27th, they "had been continuously marching and fighting, night and day; and during the whole of that time there was scarcely an interval of an hour without the roar of artillery. The men had had little sleep, were greatly worn down with fatigue, had had little time to get proper food or to eat it, had been engaged in constant battles and skirmishes, and had performed services laborious, dangerous, and excessive beyond any previous experience in this country."*

Ulric Dahlgren no doubt shared in the fatiguing effects of such service; but however severely it must have taxed his physical powers, his elastic spirit was unquelled. Writing on the 26th, he says, "*I am nearly worn out,—going day and night.*" But he adds subsequently, "*I am determined to see the matter through,—Jackson or ourselves whipped; and if they can keep us supplied with ammunition, we will fight him forever.*" And those who knew the young soldier would understand that this was no vain vaunting, but only the expression of that earnestness which gave such emphasis to his character. Indeed, he could contribute but little towards the great end,—no more than could be compassed by the indomitable spirit of a youth of *twenty;* and what was that where such a host of

* Report of General Pope (17).

distinguished generals and brave men were met to stake every life, if need be, for the capital? Truly very little, save to bear an honored, and not altogether forgotten place, in that grand concourse of heroic patriots. But the painful truth is not to be disguised,—at last our gallant army is outflanked, and falls back just in time to escape its own ruin, and the loss of Washington. In the course of incessant battle that ensued, this narrative naturally follows the fortunes of its subject, who belongs to the First Corps.

On the 28th, being near Bull Run, General Sigel was ordered to "attack the enemy vigorously" next morning, which he did accordingly; and a desperate battle took place, which raged with violence for four hours, Sigel maintaining his ground stubbornly, until nearly outflanked by superior forces. Just at the critical moment arrived the gallant Kearney, with Reno and Stevens, followed by Reynolds,—noble leaders,—all of whom shortly sealed their loyalty with their lives. Then the enemy renewed the combat furiously as before, and Hooker reached the field,—about 2 P.M. Towards the end of the day, King's division came on the ground, and soon after the battle of Bull Run ended, seemingly in our favor.

Next day (Saturday, August 30), the conflict was renewed on Sigel's left, on "Bald-headed Hill." After some severe fighting, the enemy, in overwhelming numbers, broke in on our left, pressing the First Corps heavily. Desperate was the contest everywhere, for our men, though worn and wearied, stood their ground. All was in vain; and after dark a retreat was ordered as necessary.

On Sunday, Sigel reached Centreville, and took position near the village. Next day came the battle of Chantilly, where we lost Kearney and Stevens; and finally, on Tuesday, the 2d of September, General Pope fell back to Fairfax, his advance being in sight of Munson's Hill; and the army was safely within the lines, where the enemy dared not venture.

In all this *mêlée* of operations, Ulric Dahlgren did the part assigned him with his wonted zeal and gallantry. He had the honor of standing up manfully among as heroic a host as ever sustained the cause of a country, with whom to be present in the brunt of battle was honor enough. Speaking of him, General Sigel says, "*At the battles of Bull Run and Groveton, on the 29th and 30th of August, he was, almost without interruption, engaged in planting or relieving our batteries, under the most galling fire of the enemy.*"

And thus passed away, for the time, the danger that menaced the Union seat of government. Its quiet had been rudely broken as soon as it was known that Pope was retreating before the rebel army; for, through some of the mysterious and undetected agencies by which intelligence was communicated, it was *felt* that Lee was striking at Washington. But soon came the gathering levies by every train from the North, and the streets of Washington resounded with the clangor of the bands and the tramp of regiments.

As the army began to draw near in its retreat, the wounded arrived in crowds, and at last help was demanded for them on the field itself, as the unhurt soldiers were only just able to provide for themselves. Anxiety prevailed everywhere for the stricken and suffering wounded, and even such clerks as could be spared from the government offices were sent to assist them.

As no tidings of Captain Dahlgren had been received, his elder brother repaired to the field to render him aid in case he was wounded; but the time of the young soldier had not come. Everywhere on the field of battle, no bullet had reached him yet; and he was soon heard of in various ways, active as ever, and unscarred.

INTERVAL BETWEEN POPE'S CAMPAIGN AND THE RAID INTO FREDERICKSBURG.

As soon as the Union army had gained the lines of Washington, immediate relief from the pressure of the rebel forces was experienced, though the reason of it was not so quickly understood. Two days later (3d September), the enemy had disappeared from before Washington, and then it was ascertained from various sources that he was about to cross the upper Potomac into Maryland.

It was on this day that Captain Ulric first revisited his home, after the late severe and disastrous campaign. His father was made happy by seeing his gallant son unexpectedly enter his office in the Bureau of Ordnance. He was thinned indeed by hardship and exposure, soiled with the dust of the march, and bronzed by the fervent rays of an August sun; but unhurt and in vigorous health. Of course there was much to tell that was sad and unwelcome, yet the hopes of the youth were unshaken, and his spirit unquelled.

As father and son were leaving the Navy Department by the rear door, they came full on the President, who was passing from the War Department to the White House. He drew them aside into the entrance of the War Department, and eagerly questioned Ulric in relation to the events of the recent battles. Mr. Lincoln seemed satisfied with the statements thus received, as less saddening than others which were current; for, as yet, the details of recent operations were but imperfectly known even at headquarters.

As soon as it was certain that the enemy was in motion for Maryland, various corps of our army were marched in that direction. General Sigel's command, much reduced by battle and by subsequent detachments, was retained in position near Fairfax, to guard the capital and the roads in that direction, which afforded a good opportunity for recruiting and reorganizing the exhausted corps.

On the 7th, General McClellan left Washington for the field. On the 13th and 14th of September, he came into contact with the rebel army at South Mountain, in Maryland, and the dull booming of cannon, which reached even to the capital, gave sure token of fiercely-contested battle, though the apprehension seems to have existed in Washington that the rebels really designed to attack the city.

The enemy fell back from South Mountain immediately after the battle, and took post at Antietam, where they were again defeated by General McClellan on the 17th of September, and compelled to recross the Potomac, which they effected on the night of the 18th.

It was at this juncture that our patriotic President, with that intuitive wisdom that marked his character and his measures, announced to the rebellious States the terms on which their resistance to lawful authority was to be further prosecuted: *Freedom to all slaves in the States which continued in rebellion after the end of the year.*

This was no vindictive or unlawful proceeding; it was a military measure adopted by the constitutional Commander-in-Chief, in order to deprive an unprovoked insurrection of the principal means to be used in destroying the national integrity. And it was only resorted to after the painful experience that nothing else would so effectually serve as this blow at the cause and instrument of the rebellion. It was not a resolve hastily taken, but only after a sanguinary struggle of more than a year; nor was it to be immediate in operation, but prospective and contingent upon the conduct of those who were most concerned. The resistance to lawful rule was therefore continued by the leaders and people of the South, with a full knowledge of what they staked on the issue, and thus in effect they accepted the measure and its consequences.

The resolution of the President was wisely taken in relation to events, and evinced a determination to affix the responsibility where it belonged; exhibiting a consciousness of right, and of power to maintain that right, unshaken by the reverses that had so lately attended our arms.

The proclamation rang with clarion tone throughout the land; it appealed to the consciences of all men, at home and abroad, and to their right judgment against an unjust and needless rebellion, begun and continued to sustain a monstrous social evil; while it bespoke favor for our resolve to strike down and abolish, not only the rebellion, but its cause.

Finally, it pledged the Union to a righteous policy, and was responded to; as usual, the extremes caviled at it,—on one hand, that it went not far enough; and, on the other, that it went too far.

Corresponding with the advance of the main army, the remnant of General Sigel's corps was pushed to Centreville on the 22d of September.

During this period, Ulric was occasionally sent to Washington on military business, chiefly in regard to ordnance supplies for the division, as he had been temporarily charged with that detail. On one occasion he came into the naval Bureau of Ordnance, while General Mansfield was conversing with his father, and replied to some queries which he put to him. A few days afterwards, this gallant veteran fell at Antietam.

No further prospect of active service for Sigel's corps appeared for the present, as it was now considerably reduced by the detachment of Milroy's brigade to Western Virginia.

General Sigel, himself an artillerist of European reputation, had so often occasion to notice Captain

Ulric's capability in the management and care of his batteries, that he desired to make him chief of artillery of the corps (now the Eleventh). But, for this purpose, it was necessary he should be a major of artillery, while the rank he held was only that of captain. General Sigel therefore addressed a note to the Governor of Pennsylvania, requesting that such an appointment might be made in one of the regiments from that State, then in the Eleventh Corps. He spoke of his aide as a "*young officer of merit and usefulness, who has already distinguished himself, and reflected much credit on the service.*" The application was indorsed by two eminent officers, who had known him well, Admiral Smith and Admiral Foote. It was further indorsed, and strongly, by another who had watched his career with interest,—President Lincoln. But some difficulties of routine interposed, and the appointment was not made.

During the month of October there was a lull in the active operations of the field; but about the close of the month our army began to cross into Virginia, and during the first week in November was advanced and massed near Warrenton, looking towards Culpepper, holding several gaps of the mountain-passes, such as Thoroughfare, Snicker's, Hopewell's, etc.

The Eleventh Corps was retained in position about the front of Washington, while parties were thrown out from time to time to check the rebel skirmishers and control the communications. With these the young soldier most commonly went, not being particular as to the exact position that fell to him, provided he could be of service. Sometimes he was with General Stahl, scouring the country in every direction, hunting out the roving marauders who were bent on pillage and plunder, or among the mountain-gaps, or down Bull Run Valley. Then, again, he was heard of skirmishing at Aldie and Upperville, then in combat at Warrenton; another time at Berryville, breaking up some camp of the enemy, or fighting at Gum Creek Church. On one occasion, it is related that, riding along a solitary road, the whizzing of bullets near his person intimated his being marked by some predatory rifles, and slight puffs of smoke pointed to the ambush of these assassins. At such times it is dangerous to pause; quick as thought he went charging to the spot, sword in hand, followed by his two orderlies, and visited prompt retribution on the dastardly miscreants. It was, no doubt, by such hands as these that the lamented Lieutenant Meigs afterwards fell.

This course of Ulric Dahlgren's service is thus mentioned by his general:

"When the First (now Eleventh) Corps, Army of the Potomac, was acting as a corps of observation before the defenses of Washington, Captain

Dahlgren was principally active in outpost duty, and with the scouting-parties of our cavalry. To enumerate the great distances he rode by day and by night, the engagements in which he participated, the valuable information he brought in from his expeditions, would, of itself, fill a volume. This outpost and scouting service were the most excellent school for him; they awakened in him an almost adventurous spirit of enterprise, and prepared him for more conspicuous and important deeds."

On the last day of October, Captain Ulric Dahlgren left for Albany with a request from his general in regard to the filling up of the New York regiments of the corps; and in transit encountered his father in New York, traveling upon some ordnance business.

On the 5th of November he reached Washington, and next day returned to the camp.

At this time the main army was massed near Warrenton, with the van of the enemy immediately in front, near Culpepper; and the Eleventh Corps was distributed at New Baltimore, Gainesville, and Thoroughfare Gap, "to cover the left flank and the rear of the advancing army of the Potomac" (Sigel).

On the 7th of November, General Burnside received command of the Army of the Potomac, and decided to move it directly by way of Fredericksburg.

A reconnoissance was ordered, by General Sigel, of the railroads, and of the hostile force in that vicinity; but whether it originated from the general headquarters or had connection with the previous or subsequent plan of movement, does not appear.

Ulric Dahlgren had returned from the North, to the headquarters of the Eleventh Corps, on Thursday, the 6th of November, and had but little time to look around him. Then were to follow three days replete with activity, daring, and brilliant deeds. They were to mark the career, and to fix the standing, of one of the most youthful soldiers of the Union.

CHAPTER V.

THE RIDE INTO FREDERICKSBURG, NOVEMBER 9, 1862.

IT was early on a bleak November morning that Captain Ulric Dahlgren was apprised by the chief of staff, that General Sigel desired him to ascertain what force the rebels then had in Fredericksburg; and to examine the condition of the railroad from that place to Acquia Creek, as well as that of the bridges over the Potomac and Accakeck Creeks.

For the performance of this duty, the available force of the general's body-guard was put under Captain Dahlgren's orders. This force amounted to only sixty men, from two companies. But they were good men and true, of the 1st Indiana Cavalry, officered by Captain Sherra and Lieutenants Carr and Miller. He was also authorized to take one hundred men from the 6th Ohio Cavalry.

By nine o'clock the little command, with Mr. Brown as a guide, was in motion, and took the road for Bristow Station; but the 6th Ohio had moved to Catlett's, and there the reinforcement was obtained. Leaving Warrenton Junction late in the afternoon, the captain proceeded with the 1st Indiana to strike the Fredericksburg road, directing the 6th Ohio to feed and overtake him. The party passed through Weaversville, and about ten o'clock at night stopped at Dr. Hooe's for an hour or two to feed the horses. Before leaving, the road was barricaded, in order to inform the Ohio cavalry where the command had turned off from it, and the former soon after came up.

With the view of escaping notice, Captain Dahlgren avoided the main road as much as possible, and, in consequence, lost the right direction; and, as if to increase still further the difficulty of a winter night's journey through a wild and wooded country, the lowering clouds broke into a heavy fall of snow, which lasted until daybreak, and severely tried the endurance of men and horses. The road lay through Bristerburg and Master's Mill, but being hidden by the snow, was lost in the obscurity of the night; and no alternative remained but to follow a bridle-path through the forest, which seemed to take the required direction, and which finally led the party to Garrisonville, and thence on to Stafford Court House, which was reached about that time before sunrise when the night is coldest. It bore most heavily on the jaded troopers and their horses. Owing to this, and to repeatedly missing the road, it was half-past seven when Captain Dahlgren came in sight of Falmouth, instead of four hours sooner as he hoped, which would have enabled him to capture the cars known to be there at that time. But the men had been twenty-four hours in the saddle with little intermission, and with their wearied horses had borne up bravely against a ride of nearly fifty miles during the most inclement weather; and he felt that he had done his best.

The light of the rising sun was just dimly visible through the murky snow-clouds that slowly yielded to its influence as the little band of horsemen, in close array, approached the village. An officer suddenly spurred from its ranks, followed by an orderly, and, galloping along the descending streets, drew rein on the bank of the river. His quick eye seemed to comprehend the situation at a glance as it rested upon the stream, swollen by recent rains and snow, and dashing in mimic waves over the customary ford, so as to render it impracticable. Some shivering straggler replied to his hasty demand, that the only mode of crossing then was by a flat-boat, which would contain but sixteen men. Such a course was hardly to be thought of, for the division of this small party, far away in a hostile country, with scarcely a chance for retreat, seemed to assure its destruction. The youthful leader paused thoughtfully, as if pondering upon the failure of some bright hope, then summoned the guide to a brief consultation. The prompt and intelligent scrutiny which followed soon detected a spot above the burned bridge where, upon examination, it was found that, by using great care, a passage could possibly be effected.

Just at the moment came the rumor that some rebel infantry were crossing near the railroad bridge in boats, and Captain Dahlgren ordered a party of the 6th Ohio to prevent them; but the rumor proved to be false. He now made trial of the supposed ford by crossing himself with four carbineers, and posted them to guard the passage, which, proving just practicable, he ordered the 1st Indiana to cross, which was done promptly.

More than an hour had thus been spent, and it was nearly nine o'clock; and though all was as yet well, it was very necessary that the Union soldiers should do quickly whatever they had to do; for the rebels had become aware of their presence, and were gathering in the town, whilst some cavalry was assembling on its outskirts.

The evening previous, a detachment of the 15th Virginia Cavalry, amounting to one hundred and fifty men, under Captain Simpson, had arrived; thus increasing the force already in Fredericksburg, under Colonel Crichton, and vastly augmenting the odds against the small body of Union cavalry under Ulric Dahlgren. He says in a private memorandum:

"I could plainly see the rebels gathering in large crowds in the city, and not wishing to lose time, as delay was dangerous should we give them a chance to collect, I ordered Captain Sherra to move forward, which he did at a walk, not wishing to use up our already tired horses, but sending Lieutenant Carr with eight men ahead, to gallop on and see where the enemy were mostly concentrating; he had not gone more than two blocks, when he discovered a company* formed in the street, at right angles to that up which we were passing (Main Street), ready to assail our flank as we passed. Lieutenant Carr immediately attacked the enemy with his men, and was engaging them at close quarters, when I ordered the whole Indiana cavalry to charge, which they did most gallantly, not a man wavering, driving the enemy before them through the town and back to the depot, where another company was discovered in the yard, just mounting. Here we halted and engaged them with our revolvers, they using shot-guns. Finally, we captured some thirty of this party, and fifty horses, with a rebel flag, which we gathered together and put under a guard.

"Just at this moment I saw a line of the enemy formed in a field adjoining the town, and on

---

* Supposed to belong to Captain Simpson's command (15th Virginia).

the road leading directly back. We immediately started for this last party, which was routed, with several killed and some thirty prisoners taken, after chasing them some distance out of the town.*

"I regret to say that at this time Bob Gapen was killed; he had previously captured the rebel flag and several prisoners. His conduct was most gallant.

"I now discovered that the rebels had collected another large detachment in the town, and rescued the thirty prisoners and fifty horses which had been left there under guard. It was also reported that the ford was in their possession, and that another squadron was coming to the town from below, which was plainly visible."

Captain Dahlgren therefore ordered the command to be drawn up in a field back of the town, and sent a party to examine into the condition of things at the ford.

He had now pretty effectually carried out the orders given him, to ascertain what rebel force was in Fredericksburg; and it remained for him to proceed in execution of the rest, which was to reconnoitre the state of the railroad from Fredericksburg to Acquia.

---

* This was believed to belong to the regiment which, Mr. Herndon writes, Colonel Crichton "*tried very hard to rally, but without success*." A portion of it afterwards added to its renown by assisting in the midnight ambush which waylaid Colonel Dahlgren and so atrociously treated his remains.

The memorandum goes on to say, "After considering the matter with Captain Sherra, I determined to force a passage by the way we had come, which I was confident the Indiana cavalry could do, so exultant were they after having driven greatly superior numbers in a hand-to-hand contest.

"We then started for the ford, but, on reaching the end of the town, found the rebels in a large manufactory on the side of the road, ready to fire upon us as we passed. Halting here, I gave them to understand that we would burn the place if fired upon from the building, and then quickly passed without receiving a shot. Having reached the crossing, we passed over safely, Lieutenant Carr covering with a detachment. The town was in great excitement, and was filled with rebels, who could be seen running from every house and stable, etc.

"So desperate was the fight, that our men were, in several instances, knocked over with the butts of their guns by the rebels." On starting for the ford, he observes, "We had thirty-five prisoners, twenty-six horses, and two wagon-loads of gray cloth needed for the rebel army, after guarding which, we could only show twenty fighting-men."

It was about noon when Ulric regained the northern bank with his party. He then reserved a few men to complete the reconnoissance, and directed the remainder of his command to return to headquarters with the prisoners. Following the railroad to Acquia, he came suddenly upon the rebel pickets at Brook's Station, and made them prisoners. They had been thrown out by the force at Fredericksburg, and were not expecting such visitors from that direction.

Having thoroughly examined the road, and the bridges over Potomac Creek and the Accakeck, which he found burned, Captain Dahlgren retraced his steps, and arrived at headquarters on the evening of the 10th, having traveled one hundred miles since he started, on the 8th, not including the movements in Fredericksburg. He was received by all, from the general down, with that hearty welcome to which his skillful and daring conduct so well entitled him.

There are three different accounts of this exploit, which it may be of interest to have just as they were written. The first is the official report of Ulric Dahlgren, differing in no material respect from the preceding narrative, but a fair sample of his simple, straightforward style. It was published in the New York *Herald*, and other newspapers, soon after the occurrence to which it refers.

The second is a brilliant sketch by Carleton, the correspondent of the Boston *Journal*, from which Mr. Darley conceived his fine picture of the raid.

The third is part of a letter from a resident of Fredericksburg to a relative. When Burnside's troops entered the town, a month later, it was found in a deserted tenement, and was transmitted for perusal.

OFFICIAL REPORT.

"HEADQUARTERS ELEVENTH CORPS, ARMY OF THE POTOMAC, GAINESVILLE, VA., Nov. 10, 1862.

"MAJOR-GENERAL F. SIGEL, commanding Eleventh Army Corps.

"GENERAL,—Agreeably to your orders, I started from Gainesville, on the morning of the 8th inst., to Fredericksburg, to ascertain the force of the enemy at that place, and then to examine the Acquia Creek and Fredericksburg Railroad on the return. I left Gainesville with sixty men of the 1st Indiana Cavalry, General Sigel's body-guard, and went to Bristow Station to obtain an additional force of one hundred men from the 6th Ohio Cavalry; but, finding they had moved to Catlett's Station, I went to that point, where we found them. After a slight delay in preparing, we moved, and traveled all night, stopping once an hour or so to feed and water our horses. We arrived at Fredericksburg at half-past seven A.M. Although our object was to be there before daylight, it was impossible to do so, the distance being too great and the roads and weather unfavorable. At Fredericksburg I found the river too high to ford at the regular fording-places, and, not wishing to expose my men by crossing them in small detachments in a ferry-boat, I sent ——, your scout, to find some place where we could cross, which he soon discovered above the bridge, among the rocks, to all appearances impassable; but at which place we managed to cross, one man at a time. My intention was to send the 1st Indiana Cavalry through the town, while the 6th Ohio would guard the crossing-place and secure our retreat. After crossing with the Indiana cavalry under Captain Sherra, I could plainly see the rebels gathering together in great haste to meet us, and, not wishing to give them time to collect, started after them before the 6th Ohio were over, leaving directions for them, and supposing that they would be over by the time I would fall back, if necessary.

"We found the city full of soldiers, who were almost entirely surprised, and made many prisoners, whom we sent to the ford, where I supposed the 6th Ohio to be. It being nearly a mile from Falmouth through Fredericksburg, and not wishing to run my horses so far, I sent Lieutenant Carr ahead with a detachment, to dash through the town and see where the enemy were concentrated. Lieutenant Carr gallantly drove several detachments before him until they reached the main body. Having now found where the enemy were posted, I ordered Captain Sherra to drive them away, which he did in the most effectual and gallant manner, charging a much larger force and driving them wherever they stood. The fighting was of the most desperate nature; our men using their sabers, and the enemy, in several instances, clubbing our men with their carbines. While the fight was going on, it was reported to me that the enemy had possession of the ford, the 6th Ohio not having crossed to hold it. On hearing this, I ordered our men to fall back, and, after a few moments' consultation with Captain Sherra, decided to force a passage; but upon reaching the ford I found they had also left, not wishing to stand another charge. After seeing the command all over and on the road home, I started, with twelve men, for Acquia Creek to examine the railroad to that point, which we found in tolerable condition, excepting the bridges over the Potomac and Accakeck Creeks, which were burned. At Accakeck Creek we captured the enemy's pickets of four men, our surprise having been so effectually accomplished that not one of the pickets was aware of our entering Fredericksburg.

"The enemy's loss was considerable, but it is impossible to state the exact number. I know of three being killed, several wounded, and thirty-nine prisoners. Our loss, one killed and four missing. We also captured four wagon-loads of gray cloth, about to be sent South. The enemy's force consisted of five companies of the 15th Virginia, and three companies of the 9th Virginia.

"I have the honor to be, with great respect, general,

"Your most obedient servant,

"ULRIC DAHLGREN,

"*Captain and Aide-de-Camp.*"

CARLETON'S ACCOUNT. FROM THE ARMY OF THE POTOMAC. THE UNION DASH INTO FREDERICKSBURG, NOVEMBER 9, 1862. A BRILLIANT CAVALRY EXPLOIT.

"GAINESVILLE, November 11, 1862.

"TO THE EDITOR OF THE BOSTON JOURNAL:

"I am sitting in Colonel Ashboth's tent, at General Sigel's headquarters, listening to a plain statement of what occurred, narrated by a modest, unassuming sergeant. I will give it briefly.

"General Burnside had requested that a cavalry reconnoissance of Fredericksburg should be made. General Sigel selected his body-guard, commanded by Captain Dahlgren, with fifty-seven of the 1st Indiana Cavalry. It was no light task to ride forty miles, keep the movement concealed from the enemy, cross the river, and dash through the town, —especially as it was known that the rebels occupied it in force; it was an enterprise calculated to dampen the ardor of most men, but which was hailed almost as a holiday excursion by the Indianians. They left Gainesville Saturday morning, took a circuitous route, rode till night, rested awhile, and then, under the light of the full moon, rode rapidly over the worn-out fields of the Old Dominion, through by-roads, intending to dash into the town at daybreak. They arrived opposite the place at dawn, and found to their chagrin that one element in their calculation had been omitted, —the tide.

"The bridge had been burned when we evacuated the place last summer, and they had nothing to do but wait till the water ebbed. Concealing themselves in the woods, they waited impatiently. Meanwhile, two of the Indianians rode along the river-bank below the town to the ferry. They hailed the ferryman, who was on the opposite shore, representing themselves to be rebel officers. The ferryman pulled to the northern bank, and was detained till he gave information of the rebel force, which, he said, numbered eight companies,—five or six hundred men all told.

"The tide ebbed, and Captain Dahlgren left his hiding-place with his fifty-seven Indianians. They crossed the river in single file at a slow walk, the bottom being exceedingly rocky. Reaching the opposite shore, he started at a slow trot towards the town, hoping to take the enemy by surprise. But his advance had been discovered. The enemy was partly in saddle. There was a hurrying to and fro, mounting of steeds, confusion, and fright among the people. The rebel cavalry were in every street.

Captain Dahlgren resolved to fall upon them like a thunderbolt. Increasing his trot to a gallop, the fifty-seven dauntless men dashed into town, cheering, with sabers glittering in the sun,—riding recklessly upon the enemy, who waited but a moment in the main street, then ignominiously fled. Having cleared the main thoroughfare, Captain Dahlgren swept through a cross-street upon another squadron with the same success. There was a trampling of hoofs, a clattering of scabbards, and the sharp ringing cut of the sabers, the pistol-flash, the going down of horse and rider, the gory gashes of the saber-stroke, a cheering and hurrahing, and screaming of frightened women and children, a short, sharp, decisive contest, and the town was in the possession of the gallant men. Once the rebels attempted to recover what they had lost, but a second impetuous charge drove them back again, and Captain Dahlgren gathered the fruits of the victory,—thirty-one prisoners, horses, accouterments, sabers,—held possession of the town for three hours, and retired, losing but one of his glorious band killed, and two wounded; leaving a dozen of the enemy killed and wounded. I would like to give the names of these heroes if I had them. The one brave fellow who lost his life had fought through all the conflict, but seeing a large rebel flag waving from a building, he secured it, wrapped it around his body, and was returning to his command, when a fatal shot was fired from a window, probably by a citizen. He was brought to the northern shore, and there buried by his fellow-soldiers beneath the forest-pines.

"It thrills one to look at it,—to hear the story,—to picture the encounter; the wild dash, the sweep like a whirlwind, the cheers, the rout of the enemy, their confusion, the victory! Victory, not for personal glory, nor for ambition, but for a beloved country,—for that which is dearer than life,—the thanks of the living, the gratitude of unnumbered millions yet to be! Brave sons of the West, this is your glory; this your reward! No exploit of the war equals it. It will go down to history as one of the bravest achievements on record."

EXTRACT FROM A LETTER WRITTEN BY A RESIDENT OF FREDERICKSBURG.

"FREDERICKSBURG, November 9, 1862.

"DEAR SETH,—

* * * * * * * *

"We have had a most exciting day out-of-doors. Last evening, about dusk, a company of the 15th Cavalry, under Captain Simpson, one hundred and fifty strong, arrived here, and took quarters in the lot in rear of the Citizens' Hall. This morning, about half-past eight o'clock, I observed a stir among them, and a few moments afterwards a body of Yankee cavalry dashed up the street by Adam's stable and charged upon a few of our cavalry, who had mounted and got out of the lot in front of the hall. They of course retreated, and were pursued by the Yankees down towards the depot, leaving the largest portion of our men still in the lot. They commenced firing upon our men soon after they passed my house, but did no damage till they got down to Thos. J. Berry's corner, where they killed a member of Simpson's company, named Walter D. Thompson, from Princess Anne County, who is stated to have been a very promising young man. As soon as the remaining portion of Simpson's company could get out of the lot, they were formed, and dashed down towards the depot in pursuit, and a few moments afterwards we saw them dashing up Main Street, in close chase of some half-dozen Yankees who had been detached from the main body,—all of whom, I believe, they captured, wounding one pretty severely. One Yankee was killed near Thos. J. Berry's, receiving a shot through the head. Queen and the children went down to see the body.

"The main body of the Yankees, about sixty or seventy strong, went down Main Street to the depot, and came upon Colonel Crichton's command at the old hospital, wholly unprepared, taking some twenty or thirty prisoners, and scattering the rest, who fled in all directions. Colonel Crichton tried very hard to rally them, but without success. They (the Yankees) were formed in line of battle in the field beyond Clark's shop, and remained there for about fifteen or twenty minutes, when they marched towards the old turnpike, and came into town through Sandy Bottom, and drew up again opposite Hugh Scott's, where they remained some time, and then recrossed the river without interruption, carrying with them two cart-loads of cloth which they met as they were going towards the factory. Colonel Crichton's pickets must have been extremely negligent of their duty, or our men would not have been so completely surprised.

"It seems to be a pity that we could not have captured the force that came over, as they did not exceed seventy-five or a hundred, and ours numbered in all upwards of two hundred. Simpson's company, after capturing the Yankees who fled towards Falmouth, retired down the Richmond road across Hazel Run, and did not return until after the main body of the enemy had crossed the river again.

"I understand that the whole force that came to Falmouth consisted of a detachment of the 1st Indiana and 6th Ohio Cavalry, numbering in all about two hundred men, under a major of the 1st Indiana. The company that crossed the river was commanded by Captain Dahlgren, who is said to be on General Sigel's staff. The detachment came from Gaines Cross Roads, and I think was nothing more than a reconnoitering party. They behaved very well. Aleck Green, whom they took prisoner and discharged, told me that they were the most respectable set he had seen of all the Yankees.

* * * * * * * *

"I think it not unlikely that we shall have the enemy, in greater or less force, with us again.

"Yours truly,

"(Signed) J. M. HERNDON."

These three papers, being penned without connection between the writers, and from different standpoints, establish beyond question the main facts of this brilliant exploit,—the great superiority of the rebel force, their complete surprise by Ulric Dahlgren, and the prompt attack and overthrow of the rebels in successive charges, driving them out of the town, so that it was actually in possession of Captain Dahlgren until he chose to leave it.

The testimony of the citizen's letter is quite as conclusive in regard to these particulars as the report of Ulric Dahlgren, for he speaks chiefly of what he saw.

The information in regard to the numbers of the rebels is clear enough as to their superiority, but not as to the extent of that superiority,—the Fredericksburg letter estimating the force at two hundred, while the lowest figure in any of the reports which reached Captain Dahlgren placed the rebel total at not less than two hundred and fifty men. And as his numbers did not exceed sixty, each one of his men had to contend with three or four rebels. This great odds had been overbalanced by the rapidity of his movements, and by the intrepid and instant use of the advantage thus obtained. He hesitated not for a moment in charging superior forces, and was well and bravely sustained by the little band of troopers and its officers.

The rebels appear to have resisted with stubbornness, but were so well whipped that they fled the town incontinently, and would not renew the fight. The Fredericksburg letter says that the 15th Virginia did not return until after the departure of their young antagonist, nor could all the efforts of Colonel Crichton rally the 9th Virginia. That experience of Ulric Dahlgren in a *fair field* probably led the men of the same regiment, at a later date, to prefer firing at him from the midnight ambush.

The tidings that first reached Washington were well calculated to excite solicitude in the family, and some anxious hearts were for awhile kept in painful suspense as to the fate of the young soldier. About four o'clock on Monday afternoon, November 10th, his father, still detained at the Naval Ordnance Office by business, received the following telegram:

"GAINESVILLE, November 10, 1862.

"TO CAPTAIN JOHN A. DAHLGREN:

"Captain Ulric Dahlgren, sent yesterday to reconnoiter the Fredericksburg and Acquia Railroad, has been captured, with forty men, in making a dash on Fredericksburg; the particulars not known yet.

"F. SIGEL, *Major-General.*"

The effect of this unpleasant news was relieved by another telegram late in the evening:

"GAINESVILLE, November 10, 1862.

"TO CAPTAIN JOHN A. DAHLGREN, U.S.N.:

"Allow me to congratulate you upon the brilliant success and gallant behavior of your son, Captain U. Dahlgren.

"F. SIGEL, *Major-General.*"

No explanation of these conflicting dispatches came until next day, when the following was received:

"GAINESVILLE, November 10, 1862.

"TO CAPTAIN JOHN A. DAHLGREN:

"Information has been received that your son is not captured, but will be here to-night. Our reconnoitering party made, under command of your son, a gallant charge into Fredericksburg, and routed the rebels. Shall send you more particulars when Captain Ulric arrives.

"C. W. ASMUSSEN,

"*Lieutenant-Colonel, A. D. C.*"

Then came his own simple and brief greeting:

"GAINESVILLE, November 10, 1862.

"TO JOHN A. DAHLGREN, Chief Ordnance:

"I have just returned from Fredericksburg,—all right.

"ULRIC DAHLGREN."

The tardy mail finally brought the following note from General Sigel, which fully explained what had occurred:

"HEADQUARTERS ELEVENTH CORPS, ARMY OF THE POTOMAC,
GAINESVILLE, VA., November 10, 1862.

"COMMODORE J. A. DAHLGREN, Washington, D.C.:

"DEAR SIR,—It affords me pleasure to say that your son Ulric Dahlgren, on my staff, has returned from Fredericksburg, after executing one of the most brilliant and daring expeditions since the breaking out of the war, the particulars of which you will learn from the newspapers, and from a copy of his report to me, which I inclose to you. His modesty is as commendable as his skill and bravery. I esteem his soldierly and manly qualities very highly, and think you have much to be gratified at in him.

"I am very respectfully,

"F. SIGEL,

"*Major-General, U. S. V.*"

Three years later, General Sigel writes thus:

"This 'raid' to Fredericksburg was, according to my opinion, one of the most daring and most effective of the whole war, and clearly demonstrated the principle which I always tried to impress on the minds of our cavalry,—that in an attack the sword is mightier than the carbine and the pistol. The object of this expedition was attained to the letter."

The opinion of a gallant and experienced warrior like Sigel, who so well understood this exploit in all its bearings, is well worth having.

Ulric Dahlgren was no privileged witness of the perils of that day, but bore his part in the rapid succession of personal combats which ensued, with all the earnestness of his nature, tokens of which were evident in the loss of his cap and sword-scabbard, the straightening out of a spur, and other consequences of close and rough collision in hand-to-hand fight.

Yet he seemed almost to forget his own share in the fray when he reverted to the occasion, and to remember only the Spartan valor and unshaken constancy of the little band that he led, with Sherra, and Miller, and Carr.

Old memories kindled in his eye, when he reverted to the fine temper exhibited by the men, on hearing the order to charge back through the town and regain the ford; they had formed with the precision of a parade, and as the sabers rang out, almost with one sound, from the steel scabbards, every glittering blade went aloft, as if by common consent, with loud and joyous acclaim from the whole band, "so exultant were they."

This was the inspiration *from* victory, and he shared in it; but, while yet all the future lay before him in doubt, and hung upon the untried chances of conflict with superior numbers, the admirable balance of his own spirit was noted by some lookers-on whom he heeded not.

A lady, then residing in the town, says that the clattering hoofs of some cavalry had drawn most of the people to their windows, herself among them. The new-comers had not the appearance of their own soldiers, and yet, the easy pace at which they moved, and their very composed manner, betokened no hostile errand. The neighbors looked on, much puzzled. At last, a woman cried out to an officer riding near the advance, "*Who are you?—friends or enemies?*" The young leader smiled good-humoredly, as he replied, "*You'll see presently,*"—which was quickly verified; for soon the genuine *gray-backs* came in view, and the fight began immediately.

The lady afterwards learned that the officer thus addressed was Ulric Dahlgren, just as serene and unshaken as when in sight of Richmond, at a later day, he rode along the lines of his men under a shower of bullets.

He had now fairly won his spurs, and established his right to the honor of the uniform which he wore. Previously, he could hardly have been singled out from the throng of gallant young men who pressed around the banner of their country. *Now*, he had shown by the ride into Fredericksburg *his* manner of executing an order, "*to ascertain the rebel force in that place*," displaying a capacity for command which belonged to riper years, and gave rich promise to the glowing courage of youth. He was then but a few months over twenty years of age.

The exploit was duly chronicled by the public press throughout the country, and was also made the subject of a picture by Mr. Darley, one of the most gifted artists in our country.

It is a most beautiful and spirited delineation of the event.*

In the course of the inquiry ordered by Congress "into the facts relating to the battle of Fredericksburg," fought by General Burnside, December 13, 1862, about a month after the city was entered by Captain Ulric, the latter event was mentioned, incidentally, by two distinguished officers who appeared as evidence.

General Hooker testified, "*Only a few days be-*

---

* Inscribed as the "Cavalry Charge into Fredericksburg, November 9, 1862." Published by J. McClure, 772 Broadway, New York.

fore, Lieutenant Dahlgren, of the Cavalry, with fifty-five men, crossed the river and took possession of the town."

General Meigs, Quartermaster-General, testified, "*Captain Dahlgren, of General Sigel's staff, had made a dash into Fredericksburg, a few days before, and had driven out what little force was there.*"

CHAPTER VI.

CAMPAIGN OF GENERAL BURNSIDE, NOVEMBER 7, 1862, TO 26TH JANUARY, 1863.

ON the 7th of November, late at night, General McClellan received the order to transfer to General Burnside the command of the army, then massed about Warrenton; several corps having been advanced more to the front, with the design of moving by way of Culpepper.

On the 15th, Burnside, having decided to change the plan of operations, moved towards Fredericksburg, and on the 18th the advance, under Sumner, occupied Falmouth.

Sigel's corps, being still held as a reserve, remained near Fairfax.

The whole movement of the army was so undisguised, and performed so leisurely, that the enemy had full notice of what was intended, and time for whatever preparation they thought fit to make. So they were already in force at Fredericksburg.

Washington was now alive with the passage of troops, moving hourly along its streets to the front.

December had set in with more rigor than is

usual in this mild climate. On the 5th, there was a fall of wet snow, which covered the ground for several inches. It was quite cold afterwards, with high winds; the weather was freezing and wintry.

Captain Ulric occasionally visits the home he loves so well, and in its quiet finds a pleasing contrast with the bustle of camp-life.

The day of battle is now approaching; our fine army stretches in grand array along the Rappahannock, which the general intends to cross, and carry the enemy's position by main force.

Lee, apparently, thinks it useless to attempt holding the south bank in order to dispute the passage in force, as our artillery commands it with full sweep from the heights on the northern bank; so he draws up his army on the high ground in the rear of Fredericksburg, and completes the natural strength of the position by improvised works. A little farther back is the bulk of his force in reserve. Skirmishers are thrown out along the river-bank, so as not to allow our crossing entirely at ease.

The air is frosty, and the ground hard, and so our numerous artillery is readily moved to the various positions.

On the 11th December, General Sigel, who now commands the grand reserve division of the army, moves from Fairfax by the river-road towards Dumfries, having previously dispatched Captain Ulric in advance to General Burnside for further instructions. On arriving at headquarters, he beholds with deep interest the splendid array of our army, and the preparation for a mighty effort. The general may not have forgotten the exploit of the young officer, who now rides up to report, for it is only a month since he rode into that town opposite, with a handful of cavalry, and actually held it for several hours; or perhaps his wishes to be present at the coming struggle may have found expression; but certain it is that the special order No. 349 placed him temporarily on the staff of the commanding general, and thus enabled him to participate in the battle.

Before dawn the engineers are at work to bridge the river at three points. There is no difficulty with the left or center, but the right bridge is to be placed opposite the city, and has only been run two-thirds of the distance across the river, when the fire of the riflemen, concealed in the buildings and other cover, becomes so deadly that the engineers can work no longer. The cannon now pour in their volleys in rapid succession, but fail to dislodge the hidden enemy,—and the day is waning rapidly, when some regiments* are selected to cross and drive away these sharpshooters. Quick as thought they enter the pontoon-boats and row across. Among them is Captain Ulric. The land-

* 7th Michigan, 19th and 20th Massachusetts.

ing is effected; sharp firing is maintained; the enemy resists stiffly; some of our men fall, among them the Rev. Chaplain Fuller, close to Captain Dahlgren. Our men pause not, but sweep on, and in brief space are masters of the ground; then the bridge is quickly completed.

The next day our forces were leisurely marched over, and occupied the city and the level ground that stretches below it. Upon the wooded ridge that overlooks this plain are posted, silent and unseen, the legions of rebeldom, well assured of victory in their impregnable position, and almost doubtful whether we will venture to attack.

On the other hand, Halleck, sitting quietly in the office at Washington, thinks the rebels will not fight, while Burnside, looking on, knows that they will.

And so on Saturday, the 13th of December, as fine an army, and as well led as men ever were, fearlessly marched up to the enemy's intrenchments. Forth came the fatal volleys, strewing the hillsides with our dead. The ranks are reformed again and again, but without hope, for they wilt away before those consuming sheets of flame, from unseen hands, as chaff in a fiery furnace.

Night closes upon the conflict,—the rebels do not dare to come from their covert and face those men, wearied and decimated though they are.

As the day wore on, and the unwelcome result

was becoming apparent, the general had deemed it advisable to have his reserve well in hand to meet any unforeseen contingency; and who more fit or willing to convey the orders to General Sigel than his own aide whom he had sent for instructions? The wish is hardly intimated when Captain Ulric announces himself as ready. A few minutes suffice for preparation. The way lies through an unfriendly country, and it is most important that the order shall not fail to reach. So he exchanges his uniform as an officer for the less noticeable garb of a private soldier, replaces the wearied horse that has borne him all day through the battle, and with a single orderly turns rein northward at full speed. It is just four o'clock, and by six he delivers the order to General Sigel, who had reached Dumfries. The distance thus traveled is said to be twenty miles by the road taken, the time, two hours,—a task of no small endurance, even if he had not been previously in the saddle or afoot from early light.

The general had been wondering what had become of his aide, and was looking for him in another direction; but he was here at last. There was, of course, much to tell, so, with a hasty morsel of food and an hour's sleep, the indefatigable young soldier was again mounted, and on the way back. The night was too dark for rapid riding, nor was there the same reason for extreme haste, and it was five o'clock the next morning when Captain Ulric announced, at headquarters, that his mission had been accomplished.

And now weary nature would no more. Twenty hours in the saddle, with little food and less sleep, had entirely exhausted the hardy rider. His eyes were almost closed as he alighted from his horse. Acceptably for him, the whole of the day following, the battle was intermitted. It was a Sabbath for both armies. So his wearied frame had an opportunity for undisturbed repose.

On Monday, as soon as darkness obscured our motions, the river was recrossed, and by dawn of the next day the army was in place on the north side of the river, except the many thousands who were never to fight again.

It was while our troops were in Fredericksburg that the letter of Mr. Herndon, already quoted from, was found.

On the 19th of December, Captain Ulric came to Washington with General Sigel, both having been summoned as witnesses in the case of General McDowell, who had asked for a Court of Inquiry. This detained the wanderer for some ten days, and allowed him the pleasure of "a merry Christmas and a happy New Year" at the home where he had spent so many in former days, but where he was never to spend another. How little was that dreamed of in those joyous hours!

Burnside, not willing to relinquish the hope of

retrieving his fortune, was preparing another move, and had actually commenced, when the continuance of wretched weather interrupted his plans, and arrested operations for the winter.

Whereupon the general asked to be relieved from the command of the army, and was succeeded by Hooker, about the 26th of January, 1863.

CHAPTER VII.

CAMPAIGN OF GENERAL HOOKER, DECEMBER 13 TO JUNE 28, 1863, INCLUDING THE BATTLE OF CHANCELLORSVILLE AND THE COMBAT AT BEVERLY FORD.

BURNSIDE had hurled his living masses against the intrenched rebels, and had been repulsed with terrible loss. Many were killed outright, some were left, wounded and prisoners, at the mercy of a vindictive enemy, although the greater number were happily removed by friendly hands. In mere numbers, our army had been lessened by twelve thousand men,—a small army of itself.

Another effort was in embryo, but the winter-storms came in their might, and the general's wishes to be relieved from the command of the Army of the Potomac were gratified.

As it was, no battle was again fought by this army, after that of Fredericksburg, until the winter and nearly the entire spring had passed away.

What was left of December was expended in that most unprofitable, but with us too common, occurrence of military life,—a Court of Inquiry. It had been sought by General McDowell, in regard to his share of the last summer campaign; and as General Sigel's corps had been closely associated with that of McDowell, he was to be a prominent witness. His staff, and among them Captain Ulric, were to testify, and this duty detained him in Washington from the 19th to the 31st December.

In this way the young soldier was allowed the privilege of a Christmas and a New Year's day at home. Many had been spent there happily in younger days, but where were the warm hearts and smiling faces of some that had then greeted him and lent their kind influences to the hour? What a fragment of a once happy family! Little did the brave fellow think that he too should never pass another Christmas in that once joyous home.

General Hooker took command of the Army of the Potomac on the 26th January, 1863. His first task was to restore confidence and raise the hopes of his men, which care and attention and good order performed in due season.

Meanwhile, the diminished numbers of Sigel's corps required but slight service from his staff, so Ulric employed his leisure on some device in ordnance which should meet certain unsupplied necessities of cavalry, his previous opportunities about the ordnance department of his father having well trained him in such matters.

Whenever he happened to be in Washington, his evenings were generally spent at home. Once only did he allow himself to participate in any gay assemblage, and then simply as a mark of respect for the request of a lady, whose exalted worth and refined taste had rendered her friendship, during a long period of time, much prized by his parents.

Few would have observed the rather diffident and very young man (for he had not yet attained his majority), who, in the customary suit of black, was quietly but pleasantly looking upon that brilliant scene, and standing aside among the throng of spectators. Fastidiously averse to becoming the object of even passing remark, he had abstained on this occasion from the justifiable display of a uniform which might attract notice, and yet one which he had so often worn with honor on the battle-field.

Presently he is once more at the camp; and writes from Stafford Court House (February 20), mentioning incidentally that he has seen General Hooker. His letter also inquires after the progress that has been made with his new cavalry piece, and hopes it may reach him in season. He is much pleased, too, at having observed that his brother, who is serving in the Western waters, has been handsomely spoken of by Admiral Porter.

General Sigel being about to retire from his command, which he has filled with so much honor, Captain Ulric is transferred by General Hooker to his own staff, and on the 21st March writes that he has reported accordingly.

General Hooker, as already stated, assumed command of the Army of the Potomac on the 26th January. The troops had been unavoidably much dispirited by defeat and by heavy losses, aggravated by the inclemency of winter-weather, and by the discomforts that arose from the defective communications, so difficult to remedy at that season. These evils were to be cured, and discipline restored, before the army could be put in motion.

Ulric Dahlgren reported about the 21st March, and his active nature was soon engrossed with the labor that fell to his share. His genial and manly qualities were appreciated by his new comrades, and he found himself on the most friendly terms with the whole staff.

By the middle of April, the general had brought his army of one hundred thousand men into good working order; and the approach of active operations began to be signified by incidents in the daily business.

On the 13th April, a strong force was sent to hold Kelley's and other fords, preparatory to a general move,—the object of which was to pass the cavalry around so as to intercept the rebel communications with Richmond, while the infantry would cross below Fredericksburg and attack Lee. But shortly after the cavalry started, a heavy rainstorm set in, which rendered the river impassable, and further operations were necessarily suspended for awhile.

Ulric's memoranda, about this time, run thus (at headquarters near Falmouth):

"*Friday, April* 10, 1863.—The President and lady returned to Washington, having reviewed the whole army by corps, all of which were in excellent condition.

"*Sunday, April* 12.—Stoneman's cavalry corps ordered to prepare for a move, and a brigade of infantry from the Eleventh Corps, towards Kelley's Ford. Rained slightly about evening.

"*Monday, April* 13.—Cavalry corps moved; weather cooler.

"*Tuesday, April* 14.—Army provided with eight days' rations, and ready to move.

"*Wednesday, April* 15.—Raining hard. Orderly arrived at noon, and reported Stoneman at Rappahannock Station. River rising several feet.

"*Friday, April* 17.—Made balloon ascension,—think it does not assist us much as used at present, being too far off, and does not extend the view much.

"*Saturday, April* 18.— . . . Eleventh Corps' pontoon arrived.

"*Sunday, April* 19.—Stoneman at Bealton. Cavalry from Rappahannock Station to White Sulphur Springs; river too high to cross; the enemy had artillery on opposite bank. Provisions sent Stoneman. General Hooker met the President at Acquia Creek. Raining. My mare came down. Indications of our crossing below. Large fire in the rebel camp. Reynolds's corps moved from Belle-Plain. . . . It is said that Stoneman got some men over, and, finding the rain was coming down, came back. . . . .

"*Wednesday, April* 22.—Clear and pleasant. . . . Several major-generals at headquarters. A move expected to-morrow.

"*Thursday, April* 23.—Raining hard,—slackened off towards night. . . . Two regiments crossed this morning in pontoon-boats at Port Royal, remained there five hours, when the rebels appeared in force. A small fort was entered half a mile back of the town, but there was nothing in it.

* * * * * * * *

"*Saturday, April* 25.—Windy,—no rain. Several corps commanders were with General Hooker today. Eight hundred men repairing roads near Hartwood.

"*Sunday, April* 26.—Clear and beautiful. Rode down the river-bank,—signs of a move among the enemy. Eleventh and Twelfth Corps ordered to move to-morrow morning.

"*Monday, April* 27.—Clear and warm. Secretary

Seward reviewed Third Corps. Aides ordered to be ready to move in the morning at nine o'clock. The Second, Fifth, Eleventh, and Twelfth Corps moved to-day."

It will be seen from these memoranda, that while events were proceeding to another act in the drama, the young soldier was not idle. These and his letters show him sometimes traversing the country, carefully observing all that might by any possibility concern the headquarters. On more than one occasion he ascended in the balloon, but seemed disappointed in not finding verified the expectations the uninitiated attach to this seemingly complete survey of the scene below; for the view was too distant to be distinct, and very little experience served to make manifest that no important assistance was to be derived from the use of such means, —a conclusion entertained, no doubt, by experts, which explains the limited use of the balloon for military purposes.

Some discontent, about this time, became apparent in a few regiments, owing to the construction given to the terms regulating the expiration of their service; but this was arranged without serious difficulty.

As the season advanced, and the roads became firm, General Hooker determined to strike more decisively at the enemy. His plan was to cross above Fredericksburg by an upper ford, march down, and flank and rout Lee, hoping also to intercept his retreat. Simultaneously with this move on the right, Fredericksburg was to be menaced by our left.

The move began on the 27th April. The general himself went to Morrisville, on the 28th, to superintend the passage of the Rappahannock by three corps,—the Fifth, Eleventh, and Twelfth,—which was effected on the night of the 28th, and early on the 29th. Moving down, the Rapidan was crossed at Ely's Ford on the 29th, and on the 30th our line of battle was established near Chancellorsville, within eleven miles of the main body of the enemy.

On the 29th, the left, composed of three corps, First, Third, and Sixth, were to go over the river at Franklin's Crossing, which was executed with precision and dispatch. On the 30th, the Third Corps joined the force at Chancellorsville. Deserters now reported troops coming from Richmond.

During these movements, Ulric Dahlgren was actively employed, as usual,—at one time communicating some order to a division, in one instance having to swim a river to do so; or accompanying a chief of staff in another direction; or near the general himself, conveying to him the report of a distant proceeding; but always a keen and zealous observer of passing events. The brief memoranda which he made at this time run as follows:

"*Tuesday, April* 28.—Raining. General Hooker started up the river. . . . First, Third, and Sixth Corps moved to Franklin's Crossing, ready to go over at midnight, and be ready in line of battle at three o'clock A.M.

"*Wednesday, April* 29.— . . . The bridges were not over until ten o'clock, and the lower bridge at noon. Newton's division crossed in boats. Wadsworth's brigade was roughly handled below,—the enemy were surprised, and caught in their rifle-pits on the bank. General Hooker returned at noon. First and Second Corps over, Third Corps supporting on this side.

* * * * * * * *

"*Thursday, April* 30.—Raining in the morning. Twelfth Corps over Germania Ford. The rebels were completely surprised. Fifth, Eleventh, and Twelfth Corps at Chancellorsville by noon. Went to Chancellorsville and returned at night. Met General Hooker and made report. Second Corps crossing at United States Ford in the evening,—Third Corps at Hammett's house. Deserters reported troops coming up from Richmond and towards Chancellorsville. To-day I swam the river and communicated with General Meade. General Couch then at United States Ford,—Warren working on the bridges."

BATTLE OF CHANCELLORSVILLE.

On the 1st May (Friday) our columns (Fifth, Eleventh, and Twelfth Corps) were moved out on the plank road and the river road, and were on the point of coming into contact with the enemy, but, finding no ground suitable for the development of the force, were drawn back into position, where an attempt was made on the Second and Twelfth Corps, which was easily repulsed.

Next day (2d May) the First Corps was ordered from the left to Chancellorsville. It is said that mysterious sounds had been heard in the dense forest during the night, on our extreme right, by the Eleventh Corps. In fact, a heavy column of the enemy, twenty-five thousand strong, had been moved with celerity and massed on our right, a movement unperceived until almost executed.

General Hooker himself had observed some evidences of this in the morning. Captain Dahlgren had also ridden in that direction, and perceived that the enemy were passing: he could even hear orders given among them. General Sickles orderd a battery to open, which was done with good effect seemingly. He then received permission to push forward a division, and felt the rear of the rebel column severely, taking many prisoners, from whom he ascertained that this was Jackson's corps. Sickles was proceeding to enforce his attack seriously, when his progress was arrested by other tidings: the catastrophe was in fact at hand.

The day was far advanced, when a rattling musketry-fire announced the rebel attack. In an instant their heavy masses broke in on the Eleventh Corps and swept it from the ground. Captain Ulric had ridden to the front in observation, and quickly found himself among the discomfited Eleventh, hard pressed flank and rear by overwhelming numbers of rebels. He spurred quickly to report to the general. Sickles was resisting gallantly. General Pleasonton, by a skillful use of some guns, was giving valuable aid. Berry was ordered up with the veteran Second, and nobly was that order obeyed. Our lines were drawn in finally, and the efforts of the enemy against them were repulsed with great loss,—among the fatally wounded was their general, Stonewall Jackson.

There was no rest the next day, though it was the Sabbath. Long before daylight, Hooker had reformed his position; and none too soon, for it was scarcely light when the attack was fiercely renewed. Again it came right on the noble Third, near the Fairview House. The conflict was fierce and sanguinary. The gallant Berry fell; and even the impetuous Sickles was obliged to give ground, but very gradually, and only to a firmer support; for a little farther towards Chancellorsville our men stood firm, their lines drawn in compactly.

It was nearly noon when the assailants drew off and the battle ceased.

Almost at the critical instant General Hooker had been knocked down and stunned by the explosion of a howitzer shell, but rallied in time to attend to the dispositions which were demanded by the occasion.

In the afternoon the rebel leader renewed the assault, but was obliged to draw off with loss. Meanwhile, General Sedgwick had carried the heights of Fredericksburg, and it was hoped that he might be advancing towards the main army, which he did in fact, but could not get farther than some three miles. Captain Ulric rode in that direction about dark.

Next day, nothing was done by the main army except to send a reconnoissance, in the evening, towards Chancellorsville; but the enemy were there in force, seemingly indisposed to advance; they were too busy endeavoring to dislodge Sedgwick from position, which attempt was so far successful as to compel him to recross the river on the 5th.

On Tuesday, the corps commanders were at headquarters in consultation, and it was decided to recross the river, as it was rising, under the influence of the rain which had set in.

So, in the course of the night, this measure began, and next morning, by nine o'clock, all the men were over, unmolested, save by the rain, which was now coming down heavily.

The following night brought repose to men and officers alike, and perhaps no one in that great host needed it more than Ulric Dahlgren, when he laid him down to rest on the floor of the telegraph office.

His own impressions of events will be best understood from the brief and hasty memoranda which the occasion allowed him to make.

"*Friday, May* 1, 1863.—Light rain in the morning; afterwards clear and warm. The Second, Fifth, Eleventh, and Twelfth Corps at Chancellorsville by noon; firing towards Fredericksburg, 12.50; enemy reported falling back a mile. Deserters report that Pickett was expected at Rapidan Station. Sykes heavily engaged; drove the enemy and then fell back. Meade on river road. Slocum returned, about three o'clock, to Chancellorsville; enemy followed and drove in the pickets within half a mile of Chancellorsville, and made a heavy attack between turnpike and plank roads. Considerable excitement and confusion in getting our troops to position, but we repulsed the enemy late in the evening. They attacked our line at every point in succession, beginning on our right, but found us too strong everywhere. The intention was to shorten our line during the night, with our flanks on the river. . . . . The Eleventh and Twelfth Corps were moved on the plank road, ordered as far as the Tabernacle Church; Fifth Corps on river road, and Couch's Second Corps supporting Fifth and Sykes; Third Corps in reserve at Chancellorsville. I was sent to Meade, and found him where the road-forks approach the river, and told him that Couch would support him; he said he had plenty of men there, and that Couch had better support Sykes. . . . . Soon after, all were ordered back to Chancellorsville. . . . . The enemy immediately followed us, and I so reported to General Hooker. . . . Warren insisted that they would attack us; and he was right; they soon drove us into our works, and threatened to whip us; everything was in confusion. . . . When this was all over, we thought that it would result in our success next day. The general was brave and determined. . . .

"*Saturday, May* 2.—Clear and warm. Five A.M., column of enemy attempted to move up the plank road; eight A.M., artillery fight from Chancellorsville, with a battle on turnpike towards Fredericksburg. A rebel limber blew up, and they left, after an hour's fight. The whole rebel force but one division (in Fredericksburg) said to be here. It was reported several times during the day that the enemy were moving to our right. I went down the turnpike and watched their movements; saw that they were passing us, and could hear their orders. The artillery opened on them. . . . . General Berry having made the same report,

Sickles was ordered to move out to the front and cut their column. Pleasonton was sent out on the right. In the mean time a sharp fight was going on at the plank road, by Slocum, who had pushed forward, ... when I reported the affair to the general. . . . . The enemy did not seem disposed to push us here. In a few moments Sickles became engaged, and was doing admirably, —had cut their column, taken seven hundred prisoners and many colors, and would have hurt them more, which I had just reported to the general, —when there arose tremendous firing on our right. I went there, and found the Eleventh Corps running and the enemy pressing them on the flank and rear, which I reported to General Hooker, and Berry was ordered to the right to check them, which he did handsomely. In the mean time the enemy were nearly up with us, near the Fairview House, and Sickles cut off: after night, he cut his way out and joined us. General Reynolds came up about nine P.M. . . . .

"*Sunday, May* 3.—Clear and warm. Six A.M., fight began on left of plank road, and near Fairview House; General Berry killed. Third Corps fought finely. . . . The enemy attacked us fiercely here; their artillery not used as much as ours; whenever they took position, our artillery would drive them off, blowing up several caissons. . . . . Ammunition giving out, and great call for it. After a severe fight near Fairview House, we dropped back half a mile to Chancellorsville House, and this no longer tenable, being a mere point, on both sides of which were the enemy. It was abandoned, but not until we had planned an attack from it with the bayonet by Sickles, which was given up, and then our lines shortened. General Hooker was knocked over at the Chancellorsville House, and seemed somewhat hurt, upon which Couch assumed command. . . . The enemy now shelled our new headquarters, and we fell back a little. Soon after we left Chancellorsville House the fighting ceased for awhile (this was about noon). The enemy made vigorous attacks at several points. General Sedgwick expected upon the river road. Towards evening the enemy moved up towards Banks' Ford. Howard continued on the lookout. A reconnoitering party on the left soon returned; skirmishing around the line. Sedgwick took the heights of Fredericksburg, and advanced three and a half miles up the road; heavy firing heard before dark; rode to the left and to the telegraphic station.

"*Monday, May* 4.—Clear and pleasant. . . . General Whipple shot by sharpshooters while riding along the front. Firing at noon up the river, supposed to be cavalry on our rear bridges. . . . About five or six P.M., Griffin made a reconnoissance to feel the enemy near our center and the

Chancellorsville House, but was soon forced back. Heavy firing in the direction of Sedgwick, which ceased at dark, but recommenced with great fury.

"*Tuesday, May* 5.—Clear in the morning. Reported that Sedgwick had recrossed during the night. Warren working on second line of defense, which was given up afterwards, as being too much to finish in time. Enemy moving towards Fredericksburg. . . . The corps commanders met. . . . . I went after General Warren and brought him up. . . . Began to rain; ceased about five P.M., and commenced again in the evening; rained very hard.

"*Wednesday, May* 6.—Raining. Army crossed during the night. Eleventh Corps crossing at six A.M.; not all over till nine o'clock. Nothing in sight; singular that the enemy did not follow us. A battery began to shell us from down the river, but was driven off. The general slept in a house near United States Ford, over the river. . . . . The river rose very rapidly. Slept in telegraph office."

And thus the battle of Chancellorsville ended in our withdrawal and return to the previous position. The loss was heavy, but probably no greater than that of the rebels. The operation was skillfully planned, and admirably executed in attaining the desired position. It deserved success; and if this went no further than it did, the causes are to be found in those accidents constantly occurring in war, which can neither be foreseen nor provided against, —as on this occasion, in the personal injury sustained by the general at a critical moment.

Amid this mighty host that stood up to do battle for the Union, it would be impossible that a youth just entering upon manhood could have conspicuous place. The duties that belonged to him would necessarily be humble in this great shock of arms, where distinguished commanders and veteran troops faced every peril and strained every nerve to grasp victory, and where an army of dead and wounded attested how earnestly the good fight had been fought. Still, it is something to say, that Ulric Dahlgren offered his mite with that earnest devotion and disregard of danger which always marked his action. Vigilant, brave, never tiring, his memoranda made on the spot, and letters written soon after, will show how accurately he noted what he saw, and how truly he judged of things seen and unseen; for when compared with what has been disclosed by the subsequent testimony of the actors, no material error will be found in them. He seems to have kept himself constantly near to the scenes of the great events of the battle, perfectly free from all personal considerations, and unchecked by obstacles. If the shortest path lies across a river, he swims it; if our banner goes forward in battle, he exults; if it recedes, he is not despondent. His aspirations mount as he looks with admiration on generals sharing every danger with their men; and when our right advance is rolled up, almost as a scroll, by the sudden, sharp, and overpowering rush of rebel masses, he is on the spot; the loss of a horse, killed, betokens that his duties have not been without peril.

General Hooker, nothing daunted by the result, still contemplated further operations, but was restrained from the attempt by the untoward expiration of the terms of large numbers of his men, which, with the loss of some seventeen thousand by the recent battles, reduced the force too low to give effect to a great movement.

Some time passed, therefore, in inaction, during which Captain Dahlgren employed himself in such duties as presented. The tedium was relieved by good news from General Grant, in the valley of the Mississippi; which naturally suggested the hope of being able to do something in that quarter.

On the 26th May, General Hooker visited Washington, bringing Ulric with him,—being his first appearance at home for two months; a home ever cherished in his memory with the happy hours of earlier days, and where he never failed to be welcomed with every token of deep affection.

One brief respite, one fleeting day from the sum of an existence itself so brief, yet all devoted to the glorious cause of humanity, and the noble youth once more departs from his father's door, to abide whatever chances coming battle may bring. No idle duty this; for the legions of the republic, defeated and reduced in numbers by two great battles, are barely competent to assure the defense of the capital, and to prevent another raid from being pushed nearer home than that of last summer.

This time, however, the rebel leaders will not waste their strength in battle on their own soil, but with unweakened ranks will avoid the Union army, and advance by a flank movement up the valleys into Maryland, and even into the rich fields of Pennsylvania, where they will replenish their scanty stores, and, after a terrible conflict with our embattled host, will recoil with severe loss from Northern soil.

The probability of such a campaign was not disregarded by the general; but there was still another plan open to the enemy's offensive operations, and, as the initiatory movements for either were alike, some time must elapse before it would be possible to decide which object was in view. The general had, therefore, the difficult task of providing for either contingency with a single force, so that it behooved him not to reduce his strength by division, and yet to await the gradual unfolding of the rebel design upon one of the two very different routes.

On the 27th May, Ulric Dahlgren returns to headquarters, and the next day notices some little departure from the daily routine of camp-life. A division is sent to watch the various fords of the river,—Banks', United States, Richard's, and Kelley's; field-works, too, are in progress about our position, indicating the suspicion of an aggressive move by the enemy, but uncertainty as to the direction it may take, whether a flank march north, or a direct attack on the capital.

On the 29th, he notes in his diary having observed unusual *activity among the rebels* across the river,—something seems to be on hand. There is a review of about twenty-five regiments and four batteries, by some notability from Richmond, who afterwards leaves in the cars: "*the artillery is in excellent order, but too many white horses.*"

June 4, our spies cross the river; the rebel camp opposite has been moved.

Some days previous, an alarm had arisen at Harper's Ferry, caused by the rumor that the enemy was on the move for Maryland; but, as with many such reports, it was difficult to decide whether it was an unfounded apprehension, or one of those mysterious warnings that sometimes herald important blows.

Finally, the general determined to feel the rebel positions roughly, and thus know for himself something of the enemy's force and designs. So, on the 5th of June, some pontoons were sent to Franklin's Crossing; our men pushed over and cleared the rifle-pits with slight loss, which demonstration drew the rebels in force. Ulric seems to have been present on this occasion.

Though the rebel leaders had actually begun that move on the 3d of June, which, a month later, was to be terminated by a battle in Pennsylvania, yet nothing had at this time reached our camp which justified the abandonment of the line of the Rappahannock. Captain Dahlgren notes that the enemy's movements are mysterious, and some prisoners report that Longstreet is marching for Culpepper. Meanwhile the general finds that a force of cavalry is collecting at Rappahannock Station, and, supposing that the raid is to be confined to this column, determines to take the initiative, and strike a blow that shall damage this plan.

General Pleasonton is to play this move; and on Captain Dahlgren's becoming aware of it, he obtains permission to be of the party. His diary (6th June) briefly records, "*Pleasonton preparing for a move. I will join him in the morning.*"

COMBAT OF BEVERLEY FORD, JUNE 9, 1863.

Late in the afternoon of June 7, Captain Dahlgren left headquarters with instructions for General Pleasonton, and reached him late next day. Our force was to consist of all the cavalry that could be spared, with two picked brigades of infantry, under Generals Ames and Russell, and a battery to each brigade.

General Buford was to cross at Beverley Ford, and General Gregg at Kelley's Ford, each supported by a brigade of infantry and its battery. They were to converge towards Brandy Station upon the rebel flank.

No precaution was omitted to prevent the enemy from having intelligence of the approach of this force. It advanced towards the fords only after night, and no fires were allowed. All of these measures were perfectly successful, and the rebel cavalry officer seemed to be entirely unaware of the proximity of such neighbors. Indeed, it was reported that he was absent just at the moment.

The morning of the 9th of June was beautiful, and pleasantly cool, with a slight mist curling over the river-banks. At early dawn Buford's cavalry dashed over, and were quickly upon the advance of the astonished rebels, who broke at once, and made for a woods close at hand. Colonel Davis, who led the New York 8th, followed, and soon encountered a superior force, which compelled his regiment to give ground. In a gallant effort to rally the men, this brave officer fell mortally wounded; but the 8th Illinois, coming up, retrieved the fight and drove the rebels on their main body, which was busily endeavoring to form some two miles from the river.

Pleasonton ordered this to be charged in flank, while the infantry and artillery engaged the front.

For this purpose the 6th Pennsylvania was brought up,—a splendid body of Lancer cavalry. Near the head of the column, Ulric Dahlgren, who had been acting as aide to General Pleasonton, placed himself. His own words, in a letter to his father, written just after the event, will best convey his impressions of this gallant charge:

"We charged General F. H. Lee's brigade up to General Stuart's headquarters, and within one hundred yards of their artillery. . . . This brigade was drawn up in mass in a beautiful field one-third of a mile across,—woods on each hand. On their side was a ridge, upon which was posted the artillery, and near a house in which Stuart had his headquarters. We charged in column of companies. When we came out of our woods they rained shell into us, and as we approached nearer, driving them like sheep before us, they threw two rounds of grape and canister, killing as many of their men as ours; upon which they stopped firing and advanced their carabineers. All this time we were dashing through them, killing and being killed; some were *trampled* to death in trying to jump the ditches which intervened, and, falling in, were crushed by others who did not get over.

"Major Morris commanded the regiment, and I was riding very near him, when, just as we were jumping a ditch, some canister came along, and I saw his horse fall over him, but could not tell whether he was killed or not, for at the same instant my horse was shot in three places. He fell, and threw me, so that I could see nothing for a few moments. Just then the column turned to go back,—finding that the enemy had surrounded us. I saw the rear passing me, and about to leave me behind, so I gave my horse a tremendous kick and got him on his legs again. Finding he could still move, I mounted and made after the rest,—just escaping being taken.

"I got a heavy blow over the arm from the back of a saber, which bruised me somewhat, and nearly unhorsed me. . . . After that, Buford made five successive charges against their line before he could break them, losing two hundred and fifty men.

"So we fought fourteen hours, finally driving the enemy four or five miles off. Night coming on, and the enemy whipped, we crossed the river. . .

"We are all delighted. . . . I have just had the balls extracted from my horse. . . . He was my best horse, and the bone in his foreleg is so shattered that I am afraid he must be killed."

An eye-witness* of the combat writes:

"In this charge we lost about the only prisoners captured by the enemy during the day. Major Morris was seen to fall from his horse, and is probably wounded and a prisoner. Captain Davis, of the same regiment, was killed, Captain Leiper was wounded, and Major Hazeltine's horse shot under him.

"Captain Dahlgren, of General Hooker's staff, a model of cool and dauntless bravery, charged with the regiment, and his horse was shot in two places."

The conflict continued with varying success until noon, soon after which the enemy began to exhibit the effect of General Gregg's presence in his rear, coming up from Kelley's Ford. The rebels fell back; the Union troops reached their camp, and General Pleasonton the headquarters.

The enemy was pushed back steadily for three miles from the river, until they reached strong infantry supports. It was now late in the afternoon, and Pleasonton, picking up his wounded, withdrew

---

* Mr. Crounse, of the New York Times.

across the river, unmolested by the discomfited rebels.

This well-conceived and brilliantly-executed blow was some solace for the reverses so recently experienced, and dissipated a few of the unpleasant misgivings which ill fortune is apt to engender. Ulric Dahlgren had that day given another earnest of fervent and unabated devotion to the Union cause. To have ridden, as he did, near the head of that proud array of horsemen, breast to breast with its leading files, when it dashed like a thunderbolt on the foe, was a memory worth preserving. How narrowly he escaped in limb, perhaps in life, is best seen from the wounds which his horse received; a little higher sped, and he would have been left on the field, a wounded captive, perhaps to wear out the remains of life in one of those horrible dungeons where perished some of the gallant men near whom he rode that day,—among them Major Morris, whom he saw fall with his horse. And what a captivity! Was not even death preferable to the sufferings to which our men were there doomed? Some, indeed, did survive, and were at last permitted to return home; but only to die. Others were denied even that poor boon until too late, and gave up life by the way. Who shall record all the dark horrors of that captivity?

Ulric Dahlgren had surely earned the privilege of undisturbed repose for that night; but he remembered that the tidings would be welcome to the general, so by ten o'clock at night he was mounted, and on the road to headquarters, which he reached next morning.

The welcome tale told, the young soldier resigned himself to rest; and deep must have been the slumbers that fell on his wearied frame.

The blow had been well aimed and stricken home, but it did not arrest the march of the rebel army; for on the 3d it was in motion, and on the 8th was at Culpepper, not to be diverted from its purpose of despoiling the fields and flocks of Pennsylvania. A week later, and its advance, under Ewell, was at Winchester.

On the 16th of June, Captain Ulric arrived at Washington, with a communication for the President, looking in fine health, but well rid of superfluous flesh. The errand was so pressing that he remained but an hour, and was not able even to revisit his home. A few weeks more of great events, of fierce and sanguinary strife, of gallant exploit, and he will be borne from the battle-field, to that home, a weary sufferer, destined only to leave it again maimed of his fair proportions.

There he shall lie and wear away the tardy hours, and hear the trumpet-sounds around him, and not respond, compelled to look calmly on that death which he has so often faced in stern battle. Glorious boy! he proved that he could suffer as well as dare.

Some days after his hurried visit to Washington, it was rumored that he had been taken prisoner in one of the cavalry combats near the mountain-passes; but that was never to be. Whatever ill fate might betide, his brave spirit was never to undergo the torture that was reserved by rebel jailers for the Union soldiers who fell into their hands; their savage bonds were never to gall his free limbs. Such a doom he dreaded more than death, and afterwards, in speaking of the fate of some of his comrades, he said, "*Father, they shall never take me alive.*" He was as good as his word.

But the crisis of the grand drama is hastening to its consummation. Great armies are rushing to encounter each other, and the tramp of their mighty hosts shakes the solid earth.

Rebeldom feels that its grip on the valley of the Mississippi is loosening. One hold after another has been wrenched away. Grant, from above, and Farragut, from below, beleaguer their last intrenchment. When that shall have been gained, the great river of the West will again be free, and the pent-up resources of the people that border its upper waters will be unlocked. If that blow can be parried by one as great at the national capital, or at the hitherto untouched fields and cities of the North, then is there still hope for rebeldom.

The moment is favorable for this counterblow; for the heavy losses sustained by our Army of the

Potomac in two reverses, followed by the release of even greater numbers whose terms have expired, offer an opportunity that is not to be neglected. So the insurgent leader will sweep North, and risk the fortunes of his cause in Pennsylvania.

The preparation of the rebels has been so favored by circumstances, however, that it is still difficult to divine their purposes. Hooker, calm and unshaken, with a reduced force, is compelled to await the events that will disclose by which of two lines the attack will proceed,—whether directly against the capital by the front, or by a flank march up the valley into Maryland and Pennsylvania. He cannot divide his force, or even much separate it. It may seem like hesitancy, but it is a necessity to be sure of the road they take, before he abandons the position that leads in either direction.

On the 15th of June he informs the President, "*I now feel that invasion is his settled purpose;*" but there is doubt elsewhere.

On the 18th, there can be no longer any doubt. The enemy is fully committed to invasion by way of the valley, and Hooker swings round the corps of his army, spreading them like radii from Fairfax, so as to command the upper Potomac and the passes near Leesburg, with the cavalry feeling the flanking force of the enemy. This brings Pleasonton in contact with his former antagonist, Stuart, just as he is about to penetrate the gap at Aldie; and our men drive the rebels back to Middleburg after some hard fighting; which is repeated next day by Gregg, and further enforced on the 21st by the cavalry, supported by infantry, so that the rebels are pushed off the ground entirely.

Ulric's diary notes in one place, "*Gregg had a fine fight*," and two days afterwards, "*Pleasonton fighting*;" but he missed both, having gone, as his notes show, "*with Stahl*."

On the 22d of June, Captain Dahlgren was sent down to examine the vicinity of Warrenton, in order, probably, to make sure that no rebel force of importance had been left behind. He found only a brigade of cavalry.

By the 24th, there is no doubt that the whole rebel army is across the Potomac; and Hooker moves accordingly.

Events now follow quickly. Lee is in Chambersburg, Hooker has followed him over the river, the President has called for an additional levy of one hundred thousand men,* and a great collision is impending. It seems a rash measure in the rebel leader to precipitate his army into our midst, cut loose from its base, save by the attenuated thread that leads through the valley, and retreat, should such a movement become necessary, embarrassed by having to cross a large river. Hooker is rightly

---

* June 10th.

placed for a decisive result, if he had the force; but it is the whole of the rebel army, and not a part, that he has to deal with; and it is no slight matter to destroy such a force, so long as it is kept together. Still, if Hooker can control the numbers with which he began at Chancellorsville, it is not probable that rebeldom will have much of an army left to rely on.

At this critical moment, just when the eyes of the country are fixed upon the coming shock of the two great armies, General Hooker is relieved, and the command given to General Meade.

The brief and fragmentary memoranda of the young soldier evince his usual intentness on the work in hand; he is in the saddle constantly, and, by following the scout of General Stahl's cavalry, loses the opportunity of being in the combats about Aldie.

Speaking of him about this time, General Hooker writes, "I cannot too highly commend the zeal, efficiency, and gallantry which have characterized the performance of his duties while a member of my staff."

CHAPTER VIII.

EIGHT DAYS OF THE GETTYSBURG CAMPAIGN.

FEW commanders have ever found themselves so suddenly confronted with responsibilities as grave as those which devolved on General Meade when he was called to assume the command of our army, on the 28th of June, 1863.

The best army of rebeldom, estimated at one hundred thousand strong, under a general of high reputation, in whom both officers and men placed implicit confidence, had, by rapid marches, made its way into Pennsylvania, whence it menaced the capital of that State, as well as Washington, Baltimore, and Philadelphia, while it commanded abundant supplies from the ample resources of the surrounding country.

Our own army had been compelled to delay its movement until the enemy was known to be committed to his plan of campaign, and was now, by forced marches, moving up to give battle on the first convenient ground; but where this might be was as yet a question. The unpremeditated collision of advanced detachments finally determined it at Gettysburg.

On the 1st of July, our cavalry under Buford, being posted to the westward of that town, was attacked by a division of rebel infantry, and, though much pressed, succeeded in holding the ground until General Reynolds arrived with two corps. Meanwhile the van of the rebel army was coming into action, and a severe engagement ensued. The Union troops, after a stubborn conflict, were compelled to recede before overpowering numbers, and fell back in good order through the town to the Cemetery Ridge, — a position so strong that the enemy relinquished further attack for the day. Among the noble slain was the truly gallant Reynolds.

On hearing the first tidings of the movement, General Meade ordered his advancing corps rapidly to the support of those in front; and by the next day the Union army was in position on the Cemetery Ridge, near Gettysburg. About half-past three o'clock in the afternoon the enemy vigorously attacked our left under Sickles. After some severe fighting, this corps was obliged to yield to the heavy pressure of greater numbers, and to take ground a little rearward of the first position; but the general result was, in fact, a repulse of the enemy.

The grand effort of the rebel army was reserved

for the 3d of July. It began about noon, and was made along our whole line, preceded by a tremendous artillery fire from more than a hundred pieces. The rebel columns rushed to the assault, but were met with such steadiness and valor that they finally recoiled, and withdrew from the battle.

Thus ended the invasion of Union soil by the rebel hordes, and, as an immediate consequence of defeat, they were obliged to fall back. On the 4th, they drew in their left as a preliminary measure, and on the 5th were in full retreat by the Fairfield and Cashtown roads.

The only clue to the part which fell to Ulric Dahlgren during the great struggle at Gettysburg is to be found in the few lines which he hastily penciled in the small memorandum-book that he usually carried for noting orders or items in relation to staff business, and in the letters of correspondents of the press, whose notice was attracted to him, as he came within their sphere of observation. It is impossible, therefore, to give more than a bare outline of his connection with the varying events of those memorable days.

It would appear that General Meade made no changes in the staff of his predecessor, and that Captain Dahlgren continued to occupy the same position which he had held with General Hooker. But, instead of the ordinary routine of staff-duty, he had been permitted to follow his own suggestions in observing the rear and flank of the enemy, intercepting dispatches, cutting off trains, and harassing communications with such detachments as he was able to procure from different commanding officers.

While the great army of the Union is gathering up for the strife, and its leaders, with calmness and deliberation, are about to place it right in the path of the invader, the young captain notes with quick eye the lengthened lines by which the enemy holds to his base in Virginia. Like attenuated threads, they stretch over hill and dale, flood and field, each one, in all its parts, vital to the existence of the rebel army. The least blow struck there will vibrate to the very heart of that host; so he loses no time in asking for a squad of cavalry; but few can now be spared from the struggle that is impending, and he departs on his adventurous mission with scarcely enough men to assure the safety of a dispatch.

His own memorandum, about this time, runs thus: "*At M.,* proposed to General —— to take some men and operate on the rebel rear. He, then anxious about the movements of the army, did not give the matter much attention. Then applied to General P., who ordered a sergeant and fifteen men*

---

* Middleburg.

to report,—only ten came. With these and four scouts, under Sergeant Cline, we started out."

With such scanty force, nothing of importance could have been expected; but in this, as in other instances, it is noteworthy that no seeming lack of means ever discouraged the young soldier, or wrung from him the slightest token of dissatisfaction. He accepted without demur whatever was offered, and proceeded in his enterprise with alacrity and cheerfulness.

So far as it is possible to obtain any particulars from the scanty information which we have in regard to the course taken by Ulric Dahlgren with this party on the 30th of June and 1st of July, it would seem that he went directly to the rear of the rebel army, seeking for an opportunity to strike at some weak or unguarded point of its communications.

For some days prior to the 30th of June, the enemy's headquarters had been at Chambersburg, having one corps thrown out northward, ransacking the country as far as Carlisle and York; and on the 30th (Tuesday), the whole army reunited on the road to Gettysburg, so that on the 1st of July (Wednesday) its advance came into contact, as already stated, with our advance near that village.

The accumulation of their masses on this line must have limited the enemy's communication with Williamsport to detached posts of no great strength, thus restricting their action very much, and leaving the roads open to our light cavalry.

The course pursued by Captain Dahlgren seems to indicate that he surmised this to be the case, and acted accordingly; for it would appear that, keeping to the southward of the rebel army, he struck for Greencastle, a small town on the road from Chambersburg to Williamsport, and about halfway between the two places. Probably without entering it, but only hovering about its outskirts, he learned in some way that the opposing armies were in collision on the 1st of July, for his notebook is penciled as follows:

"*Wednesday, July* 1, 1863.—*Reynolds killed near Gettysburg; fell back.*"

On the 2d of July (Thursday), whilst the rebel commander was preparing for the onslaught upon our advanced left, under General Sickles, Captain Dahlgren, still watching Greencastle, entered that town and captured some dispatches, which he must have had reason to believe were important, as he took the road himself, forthwith, for our headquarters.

The distance from Greencastle to Gettysburg is not less than thirty miles by the nearest road (Fairfield), and the sagacity of the young soldier is said to have been strikingly displayed in the precautions which he used to avoid the scattered parties of rebels that were likely to be encountered.

His note-book is penciled thus:

"*Thursday, July 2.—Captured dispatches in Greencastle. Reached the battle-field near Gettysburg at night. Hard fighting.*"

A ride of thirty miles over mountain roads, through a country covered by the enemy, must have been no insignificant addition to a day's work. No doubt, too, it was late in the night when he reached the battle-field, for the last assault of the rebels had been made about dark. His remark "*hard fighting*" probably applied to the terrible results of battle that strewed the ground so thickly in every direction, and speaks more emphatically than the most labored description of what that hardy soldier saw. For at this time our losses amounted to twenty thousand men,*—an army in itself.

The rebels had fallen in force upon our left about half-past three P.M., and a most sanguinary struggle had continued until seven o'clock in the evening; they still held to their position, as if meditating further assault.

A council of war had been called after darkness set in, and met before the last signs of battle had entirely ceased.

The results which Captain Dahlgren was able to present, as well as the information he had obtained

---

* General Meade, p. 350.

of the condition of the rebel communications, seem to have had the effect of procuring for him a larger force to operate with; and he left the camp early the next morning (Friday, July 3d), in order to return to Greencastle, which he seemed to consider the preferable point for his operations. A ride of ten miles brought him to Emmittsburg, where was a brigade of cavalry under General Merritt, who kindly let him have one hundred men of the 6th Pennsylvania Cavalry. With this force he rode some fifteen miles farther, and halted near Waynesboro' for the night. His note-book says:

"*Friday, July* 3.—*Started out early for Greencastle. Got one hundred men at Emmittsburg from General Merritt. Stopped at night near Waynesboro'.*"

Meanwhile, events were transpiring which justified the young soldier's selection of a field for his operations.

Whilst he was rapidly moving along the road to Waynesboro', the rebel leader had flung his entire army against our position at Gettysburg, with a desperation that showed how fully he felt committed to some result. He himself beheld from a rising ground the reckless efforts of his battalions, and saw the open space between the positions covered with his men, slowly and sullenly returning in broken parties under the heavy fire of our artillery, leaving many behind who would never rise again. Well might he exclaim to his English friend who stood by,* "*This has been a sad day for us, colonel, —a sad day!*"

The conflict lasted for two hours, and at five o'clock in the afternoon ceased.

Nothing of this could have been known to Ulric Dahlgren when he summoned his little band from their rough bivouac, long before the break of day, on the morning of the 4th of July; though he no doubt anticipated the retreat of the rebel army from what he had seen and heard on the field of battle during the night of the 2d.

He has about ten miles to ride to reach Greencastle, and some of Jenkins's cavalry are harboring there; but they will not be allowed much warning of his approach. The ride into Fredericksburg will be repeated, and with like success.

About two o'clock in the morning, while the birds are still quiet in the trees, his troopers are in the saddle and ride forward The east is but red with the coming morn, when Ulric Dahlgren breaks into the town and attacks the enemy, who little dream of what is at hand. A severe conflict ensues, but the rebels are finally routed, and driven out with such loss that they make no effort to disturb their young antagonist in his possession. And thus he wins the town as he won Fredericksburg, and can even hold it long enough to await

* Colonel Freemantle.

the further retrograde movement of the rebel army.

The record of the day is very briefly set down:

"*Saturday, July 4.—Started at two* A.M. *Attacked Jenkins's cavalry in Greencastle. Whiteford captured Paymaster.*"

There must have been much of incident in the exploit that was gladdening to the gallant youth, for the feeling peeps out in a desultory note, thus:

"Passed the 4th in Greencastle. The enemy's communications entirely destroyed. Remained in the town all day, feeling proud of our work. Citizens very uneasy about our being there."

Assuredly a very fitting celebration of our *national* anniversary, and well calculated to awaken emotions of pride in the hearts of this American band.

It was one ray of that triumph which, on that day, renewed the hopes of our great republic, and gave assurance that it should not be divided, nor its glory depart from it. One rebel army surrendered at Vicksburg, and the West was disenthralled; another army had just met with retributive disaster at Gettysburg, and was about to seek safety in flight.

A glance at the situation discloses the miserable prospects of the great host of the insurrection at this moment. Its retreat had been decided on early in the morning. The main body of our cavalry had reached Emmittsburg about noon to harass the retreat; heavy rain was falling, and the immense train of ill-gotten plunder, filched from the Pennsylvania farmers by General Ewell, was slowly wending its way along the Fairfield road to Hagerstown.

That night the rebels commenced their retrograde march.

July 5th, though Sunday, was to be no day of rest either for victors or vanquished. It was no doubt early when Ulric Dahlgren was again on the road from Greencastle; and it is more than probable that he moved directly towards Waynesboro', for the line which the retreat might be expected to follow. His calculation was just, and he was not long in falling in with a column of the enemy; but its force was far beyond that of his small command, and no little management was required to avoid disaster. There was a train of six hundred wagons, but with them were two regiments, one of infantry and one of cavalry, with a battery of artillery. Allowing the advance and part of the train to pass, Captain Dahlgren dashed in upon the rebels while in a defile, and, dividing his force, worked to front and rear. One hundred and seventy-six wagons were destroyed, and two hundred prisoners captured, with three hundred horses, and one piece of artillery. But the alarm soon spread, and the enemy came rapidly on the daring little band in such overwhelming numbers that escape was difficult, and barely possible. Captain Dahlgren's horse was killed, and it was only by dispersing his men in different directions amid the deep forest, that he avoided close pursuit, and contrived to reach the vicinity of Boonsboro'.

The memorandum says:

"*Sunday, July* 5.—*Attacked and destroyed one hundred and seventy-six wagons. Captured two hundred prisoners, and three hundred horses, and one piece of artillery, which was retaken. Made our way to near Boonsboro'. Kilpatrick fighting near Smithburg.*"

In the mean time, General Kilpatrick was approaching from another direction, and had fallen upon other trains in the mountain-passes, reaching Smithburg about nine o'clock, where he was soon attacked by a large force of the enemy, but held to the town until dark, when he drew off and marched for Boonsboro'.

Meanwhile, the rebel army was undergoing some of the consequences which their cause so well deserved. After leaving a small army of their comrades on the field of battle, they are now seeking to escape into Virginia; and a glance at their condition is thus given by the sympathizing English friend who just then was meditating a leave-taking of them and their troubles:

"The night was very bad, thunder and lightning,

torrents of rain, the road knee-deep in mud and water, and often blocked up with wagons 'come to grief.' I pitied the wretched plight of the unfortunate soldiers who were to follow us. Our progress was naturally very slow indeed, and we took eight hours to go as many miles.

"At eight A.M. we halted a little beyond the village of Fairfield, near the entrance to a mountain-pass. No sooner had we done so and lit a fire, than an alarm was spread that Yankee cavalry were upon us. Several shots flew over our heads, but we never could discover from whence they came. News also arrived of the capture of the whole of Ewell's beautiful wagons. These reports created a regular stampede among the wagoners," etc.

July 6th, Monday,—the last day of service that Ulric Dahlgren shall render to his country for a long while. Entering Boonsboro' early in the morning, he found General Kilpatrick, then preparing to move out in search of the enemy. Believing that his trains would be met about Hagerstown, the road was taken to that place, distant about ten miles. Reaching the town, the pickets were quickly driven in, and the attack began. Among the foremost was a squadron of the 18th Pennsylvania Cavalry, under Captain Lindsay; with it were also Lieutenant-Colonel Brinley, and Captains Chauncey, Russell, and Snyder. Captain Dahlgren, and what was left of his command, rode with this party.

The general had just made his dispositions for attack, and was, indeed, about to carry them into execution, when it was discovered that the head of a rebel column was entering the town, composed of infantry, cavalry, and artillery, in such force as to render any attempt useless. It was decided, therefore, to select some other place for attack; but the recall was too late for the leading detachment, which was already committed to the perilous adventure.

Mr. Paul, the correspondent of a leading paper, thus describes what followed:

"The party charged into the town, up the first street to where it enters Potomac Street. The main portion of the party turned to the right, up Potomac Street. Captains Dahlgren and Lindsay turned to the left, in pursuit of five men who took the first street to the right, and were closely followed. One took deliberate aim at Captain Lindsay and killed him. Captain Dahlgren immediately cut down the man with his saber, and so the fight was kept up for some time."

Meanwhile, showers of bullets came on the devoted party from every direction,—from streets, alleys, and houses. Several of our men were killed, others were wounded and left behind, and it only remained to get out of the town as quickly as possible. Captain Dahlgren was already wounded; the sensation was so slight, that he thought it was nothing more than a glancing ball, and little dreamed that his heavy boot and foot had been pierced. But he must now turn with the remnant of his party and ride for life. His good steed once more bears him from captivity or death, and then he falls from the saddle, exhausted by loss of blood. Friendly hands are near to receive the wounded soldier and bear him to an ambulance.

And thus, by the mysterious decrees of Providence, the gallant youth is not permitted to witness the better fortunes of the cause for which he has striven so hard through good and ill report, nor to look upon the remnant of that mighty army that has desolated so much of his native State and struck terror to its homes, but which is now receding, with shattered ranks, and seeking the friendly shelter of its own soil, leaving one-fourth of its number on the battle-field or captive,—the path of its retreat marked by every evidence of the signal disaster that has befallen it. It would be some compensation for what he has seen in previous reverses, if he could now advance with the victorious Eagles of the Republic and join in the triumph. But that was not to be.

It would appear that the large force which had been encountered entering Hagerstown was, in reality, the escort of the rebel leader himself, if we may judge from the narrative of the English Colonel Freemantle, who says, "A short time before we reached Hagerstown there was some firing in front, together with an alarm that the Yankee cavalry was upon us. The ambulances were sent back. After a good deal of desultory skirmishing, we seated ourselves upon a hill overlooking Hagerstown, and saw the enemy's cavalry driven through the town, pursued by yelling Confederates. A good many Yankee prisoners now passed us.

"About seven P.M. we rode through Hagerstown, in the streets of which were several dead horses, and a few dead men."

The alarm and excitement which had been created amidst the rebel host may be conceived from the following off-hand sketch by the same writer, who was an eye-witness, and certainly not disposed to throw ridicule on his rebel friends: "After proceeding about a mile beyond the town, we halted, and General Longstreet sent four cavalrymen up a lane, with directions to report everything they saw. We then dismounted and lay down. About ten minutes later (being nearly dark), we heard a sudden rush, a pause, and then a regular stampede commenced, in the midst of which I descried our four cavalry heroes crossing a field as fast as they could gallop. All was now complete confusion; officers mounting their horses and pursuing those which had got loose, and soldiers climbing over fences for protection against the supposed advancing Yankees. In the middle of the din, I heard an artillery officer shouting to his cannoneers to stand by him and plant the guns in a proper position for enfilading the lane. I also distinguished Longstreet walking about, hustled by the excited crowd, and remarking in angry tones which could scarcely be heard, and to which no attention was paid. Whilst the row and confusion were at their height, the object of all this alarm at length emerged from the dark lane, in the shape of a domestic four-wheeled carriage with a harmless load of females. The stampede had, however, spread, increased in the rear, and caused much harm and delay."

CHAPTER IX.

WOUNDED AND AT HOME.

AFTER being lifted from his saddle, Ulric Dahlgren was conveyed to an ambulance, where he remained all night. The wound had not yet become painful, but his ears were still filled with the shouts of the combatants, the clash of sabers, the ring of pistol-shots, and the cries of the wounded, until sleep settled upon the tired frame, so little accustomed of late to its undisturbed indulgence, and snatched the thoughts of the weary soldier from present pain and future misgivings. His note-book only records,—"*Foot not very painful. Slept well.*"

The next day his journey homeward was begun, and he reached Boonsboro'; but how changed in condition since yesterday, when he left it, flushed with health and hope, among the foremost horsemen in that retributive tide which menaced the retreating rebels with repayment of their misdeeds! *Then* the speed of his fleetest horse failed to meet his eager wishes; *now* he is the helpless tenant of an ambulance that tardily wends its way over the dusty and weary miles.

At this place the surgeon removed several pieces of fractured bone from the wound; and he notes, —"*Foot easy and comfortable. Slept well.*"

Next day the journey was continued to Frederick; and the patient must have been still free from pain, —for his note-book says, "*Foot easy, — no fever;*" but the premonition of coming trouble reached him in the opinion expressed within hearing that "*the foot had better come off.*"

It is some time after dark on Thursday (9th July) when the car which bears the youthful officer reaches the Washington depot, and his eyes are gladdened by resting on the faces of cherished friends, who have come to tender their kind offices. The litter is carried along the streets by a few soldiers, and soon arrives at the well-known door of his father's house; then they carefully lift the sufferer along that stairway up which his lithe foot had hitherto ever bounded at full spring, and lay him in the chamber of early days.

Loss of blood, and pain, and discomfort have made sad inroads already on his hardy frame; but the sight of old familiar faces recalls something of the past, and his eye once more beams with pleasure as it ranges over the objects that revive past memories.

An examination of the wound is made by a

skillful surgeon; and then the young soldier turns to the rest which service and suffering have made so grateful. The last waking thought is no longer given to the midnight call which is to arouse him and his men to new enterprise on the morrow. His utmost has been done, without reckoning cost or consequence, and now, for the time at least, he can do no more.

Next day, even the change from the litter to a bed fatigues the stout nature which, till then, has been equal to demands that few could have sustained so well; and the sounds of the battle which he has left still ring in his ears. He cannot shut them out, though several days have elapsed since they were heard.

Friends crowd around him to offer soothing sympathy in every form. Among the first to sit by his bedside, with kindly words of heart-felt sympathy, is Mr. Lincoln. As he looks upon the youth in whom he has ever evinced so much interest, now tortured with agony which no words can describe, tears unbidden come. Well for both is it, that the misty veil that hides the future is impenetrable to mortal eye!

Hardly a week at home, and the strength is failing fast. The heat of July, too, is taxing heavily the remaining powers. Every attention that the most anxious solicitude can suggest is constantly given. Of the many who inquire, he can see but few, among them his old commander, General Hooker: and the Secretary of War comes in person to tell him of his promotion, but the youthful hero is too ill to hear of it.

Then his kind uncle, Mr. S. Abbott Lawrence,—true-hearted gentleman and patriot,—leaves his pleasant summer retreat in Newport to visit his nephew,—his own failing health scarcely equal to endure fatigue. Before another year rolls round, both he and the object of his care will be numbered with the dead. About this time, too, comes a letter from his father off Charleston, which tells of the capture of the Southern defenses on Morris Island. How his eye rekindles with its old luster at the tidings! But that father little dreamed of the dangerous condition of his son.

The period at length arrives when amputation can no longer be delayed with any hope of saving life. The announcement of the surgeons is received with his usual fortitude. But, as if so great a misfortune were not trouble sufficient for the nonce, a letter comes saying that his brother is lying very ill in Cincinnati, and unable to travel farther, in consequence of disease contracted at the siege of Vicksburg.

Such tidings the patient must not hear. The nerves that could listen to the roar of cannon as music, and face unmoved the shock of charging squadrons, will not now brook the sound of a footfall. The passage of vehicles by that silent house is suspended, and a cavalry picket is placed near the door to enforce the order. Even the tinkling bell that gives notice of kind inquiries must now be mute. Nor may he be told of his promotion to a rank which his best hopes looked not to, as yet. In full health it would drive wild his calmest pulse,—*now* it might snap the thread of life; so the paper that carries the tidings lies quietly within reach, its tale untold.

Well, there is no help for it; the young soldier must be mutilated of his fair proportions, or else himself pass away out of life. So the operation goes on, science interposes its aid, and when the brave youth awakes once more, it is to the consciousness of his great loss.

That night, and the next day, the sands of life run to their lowest. Another day, and Death still seems to hover over his prey; if hope yet lingers, that is barely all. The mind of the sufferer wanders,—the roar of the battle still fills his ears. He is again leading his men. The word is given, the horsemen charge,—alas! there is no shout, only the low moan of prostrate nature.

The third day a strong constitution asserts its power, and hope revives. He is now out of danger, yet not fully so. The next day brings better news; the young soldier is more himself. But, oh! how wasted and unlike the former self, that felt equal to meet any ill of life! He is cautiously apprised of the order making him a colonel. It must have sounded like the trumpet-call to action. New hopes break in upon his future vision, and he seems to feel as if he should soon be ready for the field again. A magistrate is summoned, and then, almost recalled from the grave, he raises his true right hand to heaven in pledge of renewed fealty to his country and her cause,—"*So help me God! Amen.*" That solemn oath has been registered, and in a few short months the noble heart will be called on to answer for its faithful keeping. There were fears that the feeble frame might be exhausted under such excitement, but it may have been the stay that bore him safely through the further trial.

The Sabbath arrives, and with it the brother who, wasted by the malaria and summer sun of the Mississippi Valley, has had just sufficient strength to crawl homeward for care and cure under his father's roof. Both are but wrecks of the active, care-free lads who went out from their home and offered their mite to the great cause. One is wasted by disease, the other by wounds; but they have been repaid by looking upon grand events. One has just seen the great valley of the Mississippi unlocked by the capture of Vicksburg and of a rebel army, and the other has seen the greatest host of the insurrection recoil, with terrible loss, before the Union army at Gettysburg. Both had their parts in these important events,—not great, perhaps hardly noticeable, for they were but atoms in the mighty mass; but they gave all they had to give, and with cheerfulness. One had served on the seaboard, as far round as the mouths of the Mississippi; then, being transferred to the squadron moving with Grant, he participated in its action, and at last found place behind a naval battery of his father's nine-inch guns, which did its share on the rebel batteries. The other had witnessed great battles at Fredericksburg, and Chancellorsville, and Gettysburg,—alternate defeat and victory; had charged at Beverley Ford, and flashed into Fredericksburg, and brought out captive rebels to attest the deed; had harried the rebel retreat from Gettysburg, and, during a desperate charge into a stronghold, had been wounded in its very streets.

In the retrospect there was nothing to regret. So the communion of the brothers, though sad, has its consolation; and the quiet of the day lends its influence to soothe the hours of sickness.

The young colonel is not unmindful of the higher Power which has carried him safely through so many perils, and has recalled him to life. He desires to see the pastor to whose eloquent and earnest teachings he owes so much. The solemn interview is thus mentioned by Dr. Sunderland himself:*

* Sermon in Memory of Colonel Ulric Dahlgren, delivered in the First Presbyterian Church, Washington, April 24, 1864, p. 25.

"Alive, as never before, to the gentle memories and cherished tokens of other days, he called back from the sea of reminiscence every floating waif, and held communion with familiar forms and visions, that came before him in his prostration, and silently ministered a solace and a strength like the descending dew. Who can tell what angels of mercy, in mingled pity and admiration, then hovered around his bed, or if the glorified spirit of his departed mother were not present, watching over the son of her affection, and kindling afresh in him the flame of the early devotion? Certain it is, that he alone, of all who came and went in that chamber, displayed the calmness of a great serenity, himself unmoved, save when some finger pointed to the cause of the afflicted country, and then he roused into a startling energy. But otherwise he lay quietly in his consuming weakness, frequently seeking to lull the bodily pain he felt in the sound of sacred songs, hymning to himself the strains of younger days, that had often borne up his mind to heaven in the worship of the family. Low upon his back, sometimes agonized, and always helpless, he looked, hour by hour, steadily upon death, his nature rapidly ripening in a full measure of resignation to the will of Heaven, and gathering an unshaken confidence in the mercy of the Redeemer. Nobler and better thoughts filled him with composure, and all the tenderness of his being came gushing forth again, like the fragrance of mangled flowers. He now turned with strong desire and unaffected satisfaction to the volume of inspiration as to a high tower of refuge. On its great and loving promise he reposed his aching heart. The fourteenth chapter of John became especially as a pillow to his weary mind. In its assurance he cast the whole substance of his destiny on the fatherhood of God, and daily grew purer and greater in the new-found fraternity of Jesus, on whose propitiation alone he began to take reliance for the certainty of his present and final salvation.

"So, when the Sabbath came round, and through open windows looking towards the church he could hear the lofty melodies of the sanctuary floating out upon the stillness of the consecrated air, he would often pause and call the family to listen, and there, hushed into rapt attention, he caught again the old refrains of Zion, so long resounding from her glorious hills, and on those snatches and broken notes that drifted to his ear in fragments, his exulting spirit rose aloft towards the realms of the blessed and immortal! On one of these Sabbath days he sent for me, and then, for the first time, I looked upon the wounded soldier. Oh, how beautiful and brave and grand he seemed, as in his waste and woe-worn plight of fleshly torture at length I beheld him stretched out, and saw the signals of that fearful maiming! In spite of all, my tears ran down as he lifted up to my salutation one sweet smile of greeting from that couch of physical agony. That moment is one of the living junctures of duration that will never perish till reason shall be dethroned, for I felt myself in the presence of one far higher and holier than myself, on whom the mystic unction of God had passed, and made him a prince and a king forever.

"Nor can we doubt that there, in the hour of his deepest trouble, he entered into the spiritual rest of Christ's chosen people; and there, in the gloom of his sorest darkness, the covenant of his eternal salvation was accomplished."

The month of July wears on, hot and oppressive,—therefore bears severely on the enfeebled patient; but the young and hitherto untouched resources of health are daily renovating the wasted form, and by the 1st of August his skillful medical attendants pronounce him out of danger. He has triumphed again. In good season, too, comes a letter to him from his father, who has heard of the wound, and speaks comfort to his beloved son,—telling him to be of good cheer. And soon after arrives, from the South Atlantic Squadron, that gallant officer, Lieutenant Preston, who has been serving as flag-lieutenant to the admiral, and can therefore give full and exact account of the proceedings there. Such an interview must have been full of interest,—two young Americans, each of whom was to close a glorious career in the cause to which both were so devoted.

Every day adds to the returning strength, and the congratulations of friends are tendered continually. By the 13th of August it is deemed possible to travel, and, to avoid the oppressive heat, Colonel Dahlgren is permitted to try the journey to Newport. Some of his old sailor comrades bear him on a litter to the cars, and on the 15th he reaches the home of his uncle, Mr. S. Abbott Lawrence. Thus ends a month of severe trial. The climate was favorable to returning health, but a new trial awaits him here. Tears that his own afflictions could not excite were to flow freely over the sudden death of his beloved uncle, whose guest he now was. The death-blow was instant, and in a few hours the earthly career of one of the truest of loyal citizens was closed. No one had given more freely, in word and influence and means, to the Union cause than Mr. S. Abbott Lawrence.

Having rendered the last tribute to this excellent relative, Colonel Dahlgren turned homeward once more, where he arrived on the 21st September, after passing a week with his old friends in Philadelphia. Two days afterwards, his younger brother, Paul, returned home from his first cruise as a midshipman in the frigate Macedonian. He had not heard of the wound received by his brother, and was naturally much shocked to behold the great change which it had occasioned.

During October, Colonel Dahlgren spent a week with some of his friends in Harrisburg, and then returned to Washington.

CHAPTER X.

OFF CHARLESTON.

HIS wound was not yet healed, nor his strength sufficiently restored for service. Colonel Dahlgren, therefore, concluded to visit his father, who was then in command of the South Atlantic Blockading Squadron. He left home on Thursday, 19th of November, 1863, and took passage in the steamer that carried supplies for the squadron, which departed from Philadelphia on Saturday the 21st, and, after a passage of sixty-five hours, appeared off Charleston bar about eight o'clock on the morning of the 24th.

His observant eye quickly took in the prominent features of the scene. Outside lay the war steamers that constituted the first line of blockade,—the Wabash looming up grandly among them; a noble screw-frigate of several thousand tons, which had been used by Admiral Dupont as his flagship, and enacted the chief part in the reduction of Port Royal (November, 1861), two years previously, but, being of too great draft, could not cross the

Charleston bar, and therefore no longer carried the flag.

Passing this seaward guard, the Massachusetts crossed the bar, and mingled with the inshore squadron, composed of iron-clads, far less imposing in appearance but much more formidable in action than the outer squadron. Among them fluttered the admiral's flag, hoisted on the Philadelphia, a plain river steamer, whose sole merit consisted in the capacity to accommodate the large staff of officers that was required by a command of seventy vessels.

The general appearance of the land was uninviting, presenting long, low strips of sand,—beach and hillock, partially covered by a growth of small pine, though the nearest shore was denuded even of this. This deficiency, however, was more than compensated by the presence of objects of greater interest. Formidable earth-works crowned the rising ground: prominent among them was Wagner; and the tents of our soldiers dotted the intervening space. Beyond was to be seen Fort Johnson, and to the right of it appeared the spires and dwellings of Charleston, some four miles distant. Off the northern point of Morris Island a mass of ruins rose from the water. This was Sumter, quite as capable as ever of harboring its garrison of rebels. Its flag-staff displayed the rebel banner, within fair gunshot of the Union flag on Cummings's

Point. Right across from Sumter, and seemingly barring farther progress in that direction, was Sullivan's Island, lined for a mile and a half with formidable batteries, central amid which Moultrie was distinguishable. No grand or striking features, natural or artificial, met the eye, but there was significance in every sand hillock or graded outline, for each marked the site of a battery or that of protracted conflict. And beyond all was the *City by the sea*, which had been the very focus of the rebellion, and still abated nothing of its hostility to the Union.

The Massachusetts drops anchor at convenient distance, and the commanding officer's gig repairs to the flagship. Colonel Dahlgren is seated therein. The boat reaches the side, and, tossed by the toppling waves, offers but a precarious footing for the crippled soldier. As he rises, kindly hands are instinctively extended to steady him, but he seizes the man-ropes with a firm grasp, and lifts himself into the low gangway.

His father and elder brother are there to receive him. It is six months since the father and son had parted; but how that brief space has been crowded with events! Gettysburg, Vicksburg, Morris Island, tell of the service of each. After a brief review of the most interesting incidents in family matters, the barge is manned and pulled up to the advance, the father carefully pointing out to his son the objects most noteworthy. At last they reach the monitor (the Weehawken) whose tour of duty it was, that day, to lie nearest the rebel batteries. From this position is to be had a clear view of the city and the inner harbor; to the right, and nearest, are the rebel works on Sullivan's Island; directly in front, the city, Castle Pinckney, and Fort Ripley; to the left, grim Sumter; and a little beyond, Fort Johnson, marked by the huge mound of its bomb-proof. The landscape is not without the tokens of war, for the flash and booming of cannon come from our battery on Cummings's Point, at measured intervals, and the columns of dust that rise from Sumter disclose the object of fire, and the result.

The Weehawken itself is an object of no ordinary interest, having been engaged with the rebel batteries thirteen times in the recent operations here, on four of which occasions she bore the admiral's flag, and once grounded under the heavy fire of Sullivan's Island, where, being left partially bare by the falling tide, she might have been fatally damaged had not the admiral ordered all the other iron-clads present to engage the batteries, and thus give their guns other work.

Captain Colhoun, who had so handsomely carried the Weehawken through all this service, now gratified the natural curiosity of the young soldier by pointing out some of the effects of the hard battering it had undergone. The turret was marked by the deep dints of the rebel shot, but the side armor, not equally enduring, was started off several inches in some places. Some two weeks later this veteran iron-clad is fated to founder, and find a resting-place in the slimy ooze of this unfriendly anchorage, where now she rides so gallantly and defiantly, Ulric's note-book gives his first ideas of these strange crafts very tersely:—"The impression made by first seeing a monitor is that of a vessel nearly submerged, the water washing over the deck and looking as uncomfortable as one can imagine. The men show their service. The monitors have been well battered, and look leaky from some tremendous hits about the water-line."

After a full view of the scene, the barge returns to the flagship, and the traveler finds himself snugly established in his father's spacious cabin on board the Philadelphia.

A few days later he accompanies the admiral to a review of the marine battalion of the fleet, which is about to return home. This force had been landed and encamped at a convenient spot on Folly Island, near Stono, in order to train the men more thoroughly together, for landing when required. Ulric, resting on his crutches, watched with attention the evolutions, which were performed admirably, from the most deliberate time to a double-quick, which, in the heavy sand, was less amusing than might be supposed. This work was followed by a neat collation in proper service style, attended by all the officers present, and a pleasant half-hour was thus passed, in the course of which Ulric toasted his former commander, General Hooker.

The following week was variously employed. On one day he makes his first essay in the saddle since he was lifted from it, wounded, at Hagerstown. As he moved slowly on his crutches to the side of the horse, and was then sustained with care until his foot was in the stirrup, it seemed hardly possible that the experiment could succeed; but there the doubt ceased. He rose with ease to his place, and sat as assuredly as if he lacked no limb, and quickly gathering up the reins, put his horse to a canter and rode out of sight. Arriving at Fort Wagner, some three miles distant, he saw as much of it as possible without dismounting; but found the approaches that had been made by our troops nearly obliterated by sand and wind. From this fort he had a better view of the city and Fort Johnson.

The next day, the vessels were dressed gayly in flags, and a salute was fired from the Ironsides, in compliment to Grant's victory at Missionary Ridge. On the 2d December, the flagship left the inlet and anchored in the Roads. The colonel says he spent the day watching the movements. Our battery, at the north end of Morris Island, was firing upon Sumter, and was answered from Johnson. Next day he went in the barge to look at the wreck of the Keokuk, a lightly-armored vessel, which was so severely handled in Dupont's attack on Sumter that she sank near the entrance of the inlet. At this time the tops of her casemates were barely visible.

On Saturday (5th December), being desirous of seeing Port Royal, his father took him on board the Sonoma, a double-ender, which was going thither; she steamed out late in the day, and, during the night, was helped along by a stiff north-easter. His note-book says, "Heavy sea and blowing hard. Schooner in tow; had to cast her off early next morning, on account of the weather. Had a very pleasant trip."

Port Royal is probably the finest harbor on our Southern coast. Like all the rest of them, its entrance is bordered by ranges of shoals, extending several miles seaward; but there are three channels among these shoals, which are well marked, and permit vessels of twenty-one to twenty-three feet to cross at low water; so that those of the largest class have no difficulty at any time in entering. The shore-line is low and wooded, with no feature distinguishable by the ordinary observer.

The Sonoma passed in soon after daylight, and anchored near the Vermont, among the numerous vessels of the squadron that clustered about the naval depot on the northern shore, either for repair or supplies. Colonel Ulric soon afterwards made his way to the Vermont, where he found the senior officer, Captain Reynolds, an old shipmate of his father's, who had had the misfortune to lose his brother, General Reynolds, at Gettysburg. The next day he crossed to Hilton Head, the military depot on the southern shore of the bay, where he dined with a friend, and started for Beaufort, which he reached in the evening. The following day he drove about the country, and in the afternoon rode on horseback with some friends. Among other places he visited the Smith plantation, where the party looked at, and speculated on, the remains of the old fort, which, some three hundred years since, served to protect the first European comers. Near it, too, might be seen an unfinished wharf, as left by our own engineers, and thus met the labors of different centuries. More interesting than either was the old plantation-house, now occupied by some clever and most estimable Northern women, who, regardless of all difficulties, had left their homes to carry instruction to the negro. All praise to their noble sympathies! Tuesday Colonel Dahlgren seems to have spent with friends in Beaufort, where some of the black regiments and their good marching attracted his notice. He also visited Captain Badger, then there under hospital treatment, who had been his father's fleet-captain, and was badly wounded in an attack by the iron-clads on the Sullivan Island batteries (September 1st).

He was with the admiral, on board the Weehawken, and was struck by an iron splinter, driven from the turret by a heavy shot, which fractured his thigh. That very evening the news reached Beaufort of the loss of the Weehawken, which foundered in a gale, off Charleston, on the 6th.

The next day, Colonel Dahlgren returned to Port Royal, and, after visiting the Vermont, took a ride on shore with several naval officers, and saw some of his military friends.

Having thus acquired a good idea of Port Royal and its vicinity, by personal observation, on Thursday morning early (10th December) the colonel embarked on board the Paul Jones (a double-ender gunboat), which was bound for Charleston. Towards evening it came on to blow freshly from the northeast, bringing the usual heavy sea, which necessarily reduced the speed of the steamer, so that it was dark when it reached the Wabash, off the bar, and anchored outside.

The next morning rose upon a genuine northeaster; and none but those who have actually undergone such an affliction can fully appreciate the discomforts of riding out a gale, at anchor, either inside or outside of Charleston bar. The Paul Jones crossed it early, before the sea had risen on the bar, and Ulric got back to the flagship as soon as possible. The note-book gives his own impressions in a few words, thus:

"*Friday, December* 11.—Blew hard during the night; heavy sea on; foggy. Went on board the Philadelphia; rough getting from one steamer to another. Thought the small boat would be swamped. Looked '*blue*' in the Philadelphia; rudder broken, and she would go to pieces if the gale continued. Weehawken a great loss; being investigated. Large fire in Sumter. Very heavy sea, etc."

This state of things is thus explained: The Philadelphia was nothing more than an ordinary river steamboat, and used to ply on the mail line between Washington and Acquia. When the rebellion began to show head, in April, 1861, this boat, with others of like description, had been seized by General Scott, and transferred to the navy. Captain Dahlgren, then commanding the Navy Yard, armed and equipped them all, in order to keep open the communication by the Potomac, none other remaining after the Baltimore mob had cut off that by railroad. The Philadelphia was, in many respects, well suited for the flagship of the South Atlantic; indeed, no other vessel in the squadron had proper accommodation for the large staff which such a command required. But in a roadstead so exposed as is that of Charleston, and where an ugly cross sea so generally prevails, the vessel suffered severely, and was much racked in heavy weather by the sea striking under her wide and low guards. On the 6th of December, the admiral lay within a few hundred yards of the Weehawken, the most advanced of the vessels, except the picket. The Philadelphia was not only much strained by the heavy sea, but her rudder was disabled, and it was reported afterwards that the vessel had been held to the mooring-buoy by lashing the stream-cable with a few parts of rope; so, if that had given way, the steam would not have kept the Philadelphia from going ashore, as it was impossible to steer. It was to this state of things that the remarks of Colonel Dahlgren referred, and it was with no pleasant anticipations that the admiral saw his son return just at that time, as his crippled condition and unhealed wound would render the steamer very uncomfortable to him. On the day previous, an effort had been made to run the Philadelphia into the inlet, so as to repair the rudder, but there was not water enough on its bar.

On the 12th, the vessel labored so much in the sea that another attempt was made to enter the inlet, but the sea broke on its bar. On renewing the effort a few days afterwards, the temporary fixtures of the rudder gave way, right off the bar, and a part of the port wheel-house was carried away. It was now evident that the Philadelphia could not be got into the inlet by its proper entrance, so a gunboat was ordered to tow her down to Stono. Just as she was on the point of leaving the roadstead, General Gillmore came on board, and, breakfast being served, he sat down with the colonel and his father. The conversation turned on operations, and the general made known a project for Savannah, to which the admiral readily assented. Views on other subjects were expressed, which it is not necessary to mention here. Meanwhile, the voyage was proceeding. By noon, the Philadelphia was off Stono, and entered; once in these smooth waters, the rudder was refitted temporarily, and the vessel steamed up Folly River, until she reached the narrow passages by which a water-communication is established with the inlet,—a great convenience, had it not been more or less exposed, at some points, to the fire of the rebel batteries. The streamlet now became so narrow and so crooked that hawsers were indispensable for the remaining distance, to cant the vessel's head at the numerous sharp bends, the guards often touching the morass on both sides. It was midnight when the Philadelphia emerged from this curious navigation and entered the inlet.

The young soldier was, as usual, a constant and attentive observer of all that was passing, and was regularly domiciled with his brother in one of the large apartments attached to the cabin. Sometimes he rode up the island on horseback, noticing whatever was of interest, as the firing from the batteries, the appearance of the city, the new iron-clads building there, the guard-boats, etc. And in this way Christmas wears around; a season so crowded, when at home, with the innocent merriment of boys and girls, and so suggestive of the past, as we grow away from the active participation and become mere lookers-on. It is, in truth, a home festival only,—without the family circle it cannot be enjoyed with real zest. The father and son had spent many together; *now* this was their last, though neither felt that such was to be, but enjoyed the dinner-hour in quiet and pleasant conversation.

The day was not entirely barren of incident, for the rebels, perhaps to contribute to the pleasures of the day, opened very suddenly from some concealed batteries upon the gunboat Marblehead, then lying in the Stono River in an exposed position, near the row of piles that had been driven across the stream to obstruct our ascent. Captain Meade promptly dropped his vessel to a point where his guns would bear to most advantage, and returned the fire with spirit. The din soon came to that old veteran, the Pawnee, and Captain Balch steamed as soon as possible to the spot, so as to take his part in the fray. Selecting a position in the Kiawah, which would rake the rebel batteries, he let loose his broadside of nine-inch guns with such effect that the rebels fled precipitately, leaving their heavy artillery behind. The next day a force was landed which took possession of these guns: two of them were fine siege eight-inch howitzers. One was assigned to the Marblehead, and the other to the Pawnee, as trophies.

On the 29th December, an expedition started for Murrill's Inlet, a small arm of the sea near the northern extremity of South Carolina, only admitting small coasting-craft of the lightest draft at high water. A little sailing-vessel was usually stationed here to prevent the egress of turpentine and other produce. By some indiscretion, one of our boat's crews had been captured on landing, and a larger vessel was therefore sent, with a view of retrieving the mistake when a proper opportunity should offer; but, instead of profiting by experience, another landing-party was surprised, while attempting to capture a small vessel in the inlet, and lost twelve men with three officers. The admiral determined, therefore, to abate the nuisance, and the satisfaction of the rebels at this double mishap, by sending a suitable force to do the work. Two gunboats (Nipsic and Sanford), with two very light-draft steamers, and two sailing-vessels, were directed to prepare for the expedition; four howitzers and one hundred marines were added, the whole under Captain Joseph Green.

As soon as Colonel Dahlgren perceived that the measure was contemplated, he became desirous to join it, and to command the landing force. This was not possible, however, as he was an army officer, and, besides, his crippled condition would interfere with the personal exertion required to land on an open sea-beach; but, to quiet his anxiety, his father permitted him to embark as a volunteer. So, on the afternoon of the 29th, he repaired to the Nipsic, and late in the day the little squadron steamed off in a northerly direction.

His own account of the operation is thus briefly recorded:

"*Wednesday, December* 30.—Beautiful weather, wind northwestward. Arrived in the afternoon off Murrill's Inlet. Ethan Allen and Maugham came up. Wind shifting to northeast. Clouding over. Good fishing. Preparations for landing complete. Everybody eager to take part. The pilot, Prince, quite a character. Went to bed. In the night heavy sea arose. Ship rolled a great deal.

"*Thursday, December* 31.—Rough and rainy,—wind northeast. Heavy sea during last night. Moved off Georgetown. Wind coming to southwest. During the gale, last night, a boat got adrift, and the tug was much strained. Guns, etc. taken out of boats. Refugees report that the rebels expected us, and had reinforcements from Savannah and Georgetown waiting for us.

"*Friday, January* 1, 1864.—High wind southwest. Sandford started home. Nipsic went to Murrill's Inlet,—opened fire on the schooner. Four boats landed with marines. Very pretty as the boats shoved off,—hard pulling,—landed successfully. Schooner in flames,—very black smoke from one hundred and nineteen barrels of turpentine. Two hundred cavalry came down,—a happy New Year doubtless to them."

Having thus accomplished the purpose, the Nipsic (Captain Spotts) returned to Charleston, and Ulric resumed his place in his father's cabin. Here he passed part of the time in reading, or in observing surrounding objects from the cabin windows: sometimes in exercising outside in the open air, or in spending an hour with the officers of the staff. If the weather was suitable, a ride on horseback varied the occupation of the passing hours, or a pull in the fine, roomy barge, which the stout arms of more than a dozen seamen drove swiftly over the toppling seas. The subject always present to him, however, was the pending military and naval prospect, of which there was no closer observer there. His eye never failed to notice any changes that might occur, and, notwithstanding his disability and as yet unconfirmed health, he even joined the scouting-parties that went up at night to reconnoiter the rebel movements at the front. As the Philadelphia was still in a disabled condition, the admiral generally left that vessel before sundown, and passed the night in one of the gunboats, among the iron-clads, that were anchored well up the roads on blockade, and in readiness also to support the picket-monitors if attacked. Being detained later than usual by business, one evening, it was quite dark before he got over the inlet bar, and pulled alongside a tug in order to steam up with more facility. It was a stormy-looking January night, the sea was rough, and a light rain was falling. Scrambling over the side of the little steamer as well as the motion permitted, the admiral unexpectedly encountered his son, very composedly steadying himself on his crutches against the cabin bulkhead. He was bound up to the front with the scouting officer, to pass part of that inclement night in watching the enemy's movements.

On the 12th, he attended a flag-raising at Fort Wagner, when the Union banner was displayed from a pole of very commanding height. Speeches were made, etc., and it was supposed that the rebels would join in celebrating the occasion by opening fire, but they did not.

On the 16th of January, General Gillmore visited the admiral, and Colonel Dahlgren notes some of the conversation that passed, which happened to be of more than usual interest.

On the 20th, he mentions a review by General Gordon, of the troops under his command, and remarks their good appearance.

And now the hour drew near when father and

son were to part for the last time. Ulric's wound was healing rapidly, and his crippled limb becoming firm enough to bear artificial assistance, which was best to be obtained by returning North. It was therefore decided on, with the understanding that when the new monitors should arrive Colonel Dahlgren would return, and be allowed to accompany the fleet into the harbor.

The supply-ship had come in early from the southward, and anchored off the inlet for more convenient access to the flagship. About four o'clock, Ulric Dahlgren stood in the gangway of the Philadelphia, resting on his crutches, and bade adieu to many friends who had met there for that purpose. In his hand was a small box, containing a valued memorial of hard service. As he grasps the man-rope to descend into the unsteady boat, many kind hands are stretched forth to aid the crippled soldier. The oars are dropped into the water, and, as the barge glides away, the young officer raises his cap in friendly farewell to his naval comrades.

The sun of the short day is rapidly descending to the horizon, the tide swells full on the bar, and the anchor of the steamer is nearly atrip. On the quarter-deck the admiral is exchanging some parting words with his beloved son, little thinking that they are to be the last on this side of eternity, and unheeding the impatience of the captain, who is most anxious that he shall have sufficient daylight and water to get into the open sea. But the last moment together has been spent. Father and son exchange the farewell greeting, and are separated *forever.*

As the barge glides away from the departing steamer, the admiral turns and waves his cap to his son in affectionate adieu, until the forms of both become indistinct in the distance.

The steamer rapidly crosses the bar, and is soon on the broad ocean.

And thus concludes another of the few chapters, in the life of Ulric Dahlgren.

CHAPTER XI.

ATTEMPT TO RESCUE THE UNION SOLDIERS FROM CAPTIVITY AT LIBBY AND BELLE ISLE, IN RICHMOND.

AFTER a pleasant run of fifty hours, the steamer reached Fortress Monroe about dark of January 24th (Sunday).

Many lights were glittering ashore, and on board the fleet of vessels at anchor in the roads. The moon was rising in all the majesty of a full orb, and disclosed the dim outlines of objects on land and water. Upon this mingled scene of loveliness, the young man stood gazing and rapt in contemplation, until the anchor was dropped and the steamer swung round to the tide; then he hastened to the flagship and paid his respects to Admiral Lee. During the night the voyage was resumed, and next day the steamer entered the Delaware, arriving at the Philadelphia Navy Yard about midnight.

On Tuesday (26th June, 1864) Colonel Dahlgren took the train for Washington, and that evening he reached home *once more.*

During the three weeks that followed, he occupied himself in returning the calls and acknowledging the attentions of friends who had been so kind while he was the inmate of a sick-chamber; he also paid his respects to the principal officers of the government,—and wherever he went was received with the warmest welcome. He was constantly the object of flattering notice, and the impression he made on all who met him was that of an unobtrusive and modest young man, whose thoughts were earnestly and enthusiastically bent on the future of his country.

The project of an expedition to rescue the Union soldiers from the horrible dungeons of Richmond, where they were immured, reached him about this time.

"The idea originated with General Kilpatrick, and, on being submitted in all its details, met the approbation of the Secretary of War, and of the President of the United States."*

The cruel usage to which our brave men were subjected in these prisons had attracted much attention at the North, arousing the warmest feelings for their sufferings, and the deepest indignation against those who inflicted them. All this is now a matter of history, not to be denied or extenuated, for the stamp of judicial decision has given certainty to the strongest allegations; and at least one

* Memoir of General Kilpatrick, by Dr. Moore.

of the infamous jailers has found a fitting end at the hands of the hangman for his share in these atrocities.

This state of things had existed at Richmond from an early period of the rebellion, and had conferred a notoriety on its *Bastilles* which will never pass away. There was not the least attempt to disguise the fact. On the contrary, the existence of Libby and Belle Isle, and the wretched condition of our men who were confined there, were as well known outside as to the unfortunate victims themselves, who, in filth, and want, and disease, were suffering all that neglect or vengeance could inflict.

Neither the entreaties nor the denunciations of the Union government or people could shake the fell purpose of those who perpetrated or permitted the enormity. It went on increasing and extending until the infamous pens of Salisbury, and Florence, and Andersonville became as abhorrent as the dungeons of Richmond; but with this difference, that at Richmond the rebel authorities themselves could not fail to be witnesses of these atrocities. That city supplied high places for these officials, as well as dungeons for Union soldiers, and graves for the victims. Within its fortifications were gathered the first dignitaries of rebeldom, as well as the gallant sons of the North whose sad fate it had been to become their captives. The inhuman treatment to which the latter were subjected could not by any possibility have been unknown to the former, for it occurred almost in their presence; and the anguish it inflicted on loyal hearts was wafted to Southern ears on every breeze. The cry of parents, wives, and children was mingled with the wail of the widow and the orphan. But all in vain. If the leaders did not of themselves deny food and clothing and space to the wants of existence, they permitted their wretched subordinates to do so, and lived in view of the dungeons where the sad wrecks of humanity that had escaped rebel steel and bullet were being slowly consumed by equally fatal but more terrible means. They could hardly avoid seeing the prison-bars, which our men dared not approach, if only for a breath of the pure air of heaven, except at the risk of being shot down. The tidings of such horrid barbarity were carried to the North daily, and entered our homes as if the first-born had been marked by the destroying angel.

Among our youth, no one had been more painfully impressed with a keen sense of this revolting atrocity than Ulric Dahlgren. It awakened his deepest indignation. War in its mildest form is cruel enough to sate a tiger, and he had ever been most careful to avoid aggravating these sorrows by inflicting needless pain on any. Little was there of the country between the capital and the Rappahannock that he had not traversed by day and by night as a soldier of the Union,—along its roads and lanes, over mountain, hill, and dale, through forest, and field, and villages, and past the farm-houses of a people avowedly hostile to *the cause*, who never hesitated to exhibit their feelings and their resentment upon every occasion. In the succession of fierce battles that pushed the army under Pope back to the very lines of Washington, he had done his part as a good soldier. At Fredericksburg, and Chancellorsville, and Gettysburg, he was among the foremost who thronged around our banner in its hour of greatest danger. His own exploits at Fredericksburg, and Greencastle, and Hagerstown will not soon be forgotten. He knew, too, what it was to face the bullet of the assassin as well as the shock of open war, and had been marked for death more than once by the murderous marauders that infested the solitary paths of the country. But none of these had ever provoked him to vengeance on defenseless prisoners, or rendered him unmindful of the claims of women and children. He was ever kind and gentle to their helplessness, and in no single instance did they or their little property ever suffer at his hands. An undrawn month's pay was all of this world's goods that the noble youth left behind him.

But his kindly nature was agitated beyond bounds by the unprovoked and persistent barbarities inflicted in the cells of Richmond. When visiting his father off Charleston, he often adverted to them in unsparing terms. He looked upon them as violations of all law, human and divine, and liable to punishment by the same merciless code that they invoked.

On his return North, he was no sooner apprised that the object of the contemplated expedition was to release the Union soldiers confined at Richmond, than he eagerly sought to join it.

It was well known that he was in no condition to take the field just then; for, the maimed limb not being yet healed, he moved on crutches, and his emaciated frame gave token of unrestored vigor; wherefore his friends strove to dissuade him from the undertaking. But the remembrance of comrades pining in loathsome dungeons, and a painful conviction of the sufferings of men with whom he had shared the privation of the camp and the danger of the scout and the skirmish, and with whom he had ridden side by side in the daring charge at Beverley Ford, and other well-fought fields, animated every pulse of his gallant heart. He felt that duty called him to some effort in their behalf, and, disregarding every consideration of self, he hesitated not to incur any hardship or danger for their relief.

Of him it may be truly said, as it was of another, that "Never did Christian knight of old ride forth to battle with the fierce infidel on the plains of Palestine, with purer, holier purpose, unmixed with self or self-interest, than did he, who risked life, liberty, and fame to give freedom to others."

On the 18th February, 1864, Ulric Dahlgren left Washington, and, taking the Alexandria cars, reached Brandy Station. There he mounted his horse and rode to General Kilpatrick's headquarters, at Stevensburg, some five miles farther. Here he found himself amid scenes very suggestive of past events in the campaigns of Generals Pope and Hooker; and not far to the northward was Beverley Ford, where he had escaped so narrowly from death or captivity in the previous year.

Ten days were passed in arranging and completing details, during which time Colonel Dahlgren was in daily consultation with the general upon all that concerned the expedition.

The entire force was to be composed of cavalry, amounting to about four thousand men, of which Ulric Dahlgren was to command an independent column of five hundred men, selected from all the regiments. With this column he was to diverge from the route of the main body, and, after effecting certain purposes, rejoin it at or near Richmond, all entering the city together.

On the 28th of February (Sunday) the expedition moved on its destination.

But before committing himself to the desperate chances of the task, the young soldier did not forget his duty to his remaining parent, in which he had never failed during his whole life; and now that he was about to risk that life so calmly for a solemn purpose, he felt that it behooved him to leave behind a farewell to his father, in case the worst should befall him.

He wrote as follows:

"HEADQUARTERS THIRD DIVISION CAVALRY CORPS,
STEVENSBURG, Feb. 26, 1864.

"DEAR FATHER,—I have not returned to the fleet, because there is a grand raid to be made, and I am to have a very important command. If successful, it will be the grandest thing on record; and if it fails, many of us will '*go up.*' I may be captured, or I may be '*tumbled over;*' but it is an undertaking that if I were not in, I should be ashamed to show my face again. With such an important command, I am afraid to mention it, for fear this letter might fall into wrong hands before reaching you. I find that I can stand the service perfectly well without my leg. I think we will be successful, although a desperate undertaking.

"Aunt Patty can tell you, when you return. I will write you more fully when we return. If we do not return, there is no better place to '*give up the ghost.*'

"Your affectionate son,
"ULRIC DAHLGREN."

Ulric Dahlgren took the advance with his column, just as the night was closing in. The route lay across the Rapidan, by Ely's Ford, where it was known that the rebels had a strong picket; this it was indispensable to capture without giving alarm to a superior force of the enemy, not far distant. And it was accomplished by a detachment under the guidance of Mr. Hogan, the skillful and daring scout, well known to Colonel Dahlgren, and whom he had selected to pioneer the march. The Union column was thus enabled to cross the ford unperceived.

Through the night the sky was dark and the weather unsettled, but it did not rain, and the column traveled onward rapidly, halting next morning at a stream for the ambulances, which, after crossing, ascended slowly the steep bank.

Ulric Dahlgren made use of the opportunity to look at his men, so they were formed for this purpose, and he rode twice along the line. An officer who was present writes, "*Many had never seen him before. His appearance, however, gave general satisfaction, and expressions of confidence were heard all around.*"

After this brief halt, the march was resumed, and continued steadily, with the exception of one stoppage, in the morning, to feed.

About two or three o'clock in the afternoon, Colonel Dahlgren struck the railroad (Virginia

Central) about a mile below Fredericshall Station, to which he rode. A party of rebel officers who were crossing the woods, little suspecting the presence of Union soldiers, were all captured; some were released and a few retained, among the latter Captain Dement.

The column now proceeded some five miles along the road, and tore up half a mile of the rails, cut the telegraphic wire, and, quitting the track, turned off southerly, crossing the South Anna an hour before dark.

About ten o'clock in the evening the rain, which had been threatening all day, came down heavily, continuing through the night. Such protracted marching and severe exposure might well tax the endurance of even the hardy troopers; but, as one who shared in it writes, "*Who could complain of weariness when he looked at the colonel, still weak from his wound, riding along quietly, uncomplainingly, ever vigilantly watching every incident of the march?*"

It was nearly midnight when the jaded column reached a small grocery-store that stood near the roadside. Drenched with rain, but unquelled in spirit, and as cheerful as if not exposed to the inclemency of a February night, the young soldier was assisted to alight from his horse. In reply to a kind inquiry whether he was not fatigued, he said, "*We'll have some supper and two hours' sleep, then you'll see how bright I am.*"

So the weary men and horses betook themselves to such fare and repose as the time allowed.

Next morning (Tuesday, March 1) every man was in the saddle by daylight, and moved forward, notwithstanding the dismal weather, for the rain was still coming down; but about seven o'clock it ceased, and the sky showed signs of clearing off. About ten o'clock the column reached the canal, and, after cutting it, followed its general direction for some distance. At Mannakin Town, an effort was made to cross the James River by fording, under the guidance of a negro, but it was too deep, and the design to approach Richmond by the southern bank failed.

Colonel Dahlgren struck the plank road about one o'clock in the afternoon, and followed it until three o'clock, when some rebel pickets were encountered, and driven back after some sharp firing. Diverging here from the plank road, he began to approach the city more directly.

By this time, both men and horses stood in need of some respite. A halt was therefore ordered when nearly dark, and such a meal taken as the circumstances permitted; this occurred about eight miles from Richmond.

The thoughts of the youthful leader were, however, intent on a graver matter. Not a token yet greeted eye or ear of the presence of the main body, though he was quite near enough to the scene of action to detect either, if Kilpatrick were at hand. Should the junction fail, then was he left to his own resources, with a mere handful of wearied men, in the midst of a hostile country, and so near the chief rebel stronghold that even to extricate his command from such a critical situation would become difficult as soon as it was discovered. It was evident that he felt assured at this time of the failure to connect with the main force, and, therefore, that the expedition was not to succeed; for at the scanty meal just taken, he expressed his disappointment at not having some sign of the presence of the general; but, "*so quietly was this said*," writes an officer, "*that, but for a sad glance from his eye, one would not have known how much he felt it.*"

It behooved Ulric Dahlgren, therefore, to take such measures as might look solely to a reliance on himself and the force which he had, and he proceeded on this assumption with his usual spirit and promptness. It might have been possible to withdraw and retrace his steps with comparative security; but this course ill suited with his temper or judgment. Moreover, he felt bound in honor to ascertain beyond peradventure that the main body was not somewhere in the vicinity of the city.

The order was therefore given to move on, and about dark the little band of Union horsemen was riding forward directly upon Richmond.

As a friend assisted him to mount, he remarked,

with his accustomed cheerfulness, on the awkwardness of his crippled limb, and added, "*We are going on; and if we succeed, I'd gladly lose the other.*"

Our cavalry was soon so close to Richmond as to come in contact with some rebel infantry posted in the advanced works; for Kilpatrick had appeared in the morning, and caused the wildest alarm throughout the whole city.

At this moment, far away from all succor, with only a small force of troopers, and hardly more than a gunshot from the stronghold of rebeldom, the splendid courage of the young leader had never blazed forth more brightly.

One who was near him says, "*The skirmishing was heavy, the enemy's fire very annoying; but I stopped, in admiration of the colonel's coolness. He rode along the line, speaking to the men, so calm, so quiet, so brave, that it seemed to me the veriest coward must needs fight, if never before.*"

Then came the charge, Ulric Dahlgren among the foremost, scattering the enemy and driving them into their works.

Nothing more remained to be done except to ride on and endeavor to gain the Union lines below.

The night was dark, the rain fell in torrents, the storm beat into the faces of the wearied troopers, and even their cloaks were stiffened with sleet. They had been in their saddles, with little intermission, for three days. Ulric Dahlgren himself rode with the advance, about one hundred strong, leaving at intervals pickets on white horses to mark the course taken;* but, notwithstanding this precaution, the main body became separated from the advance, and thus the gallant youth was left to his fate. At what time the separation occurred seems to have been entirely unknown, owing to the severity of the storm.

Through the whole dreary night, rapidly onward rode the little Union party.

WEDNESDAY, MARCH 2, THE LAST DAY OF A GLORIOUS LIFE.

The heavy clouds of the night were fast breaking in the east, and the pelting rain, which had drenched and chilled the men and horses all night, was now ceasing. It was a wintry morning, and the genial influence of the sun was yet unfelt. The situation might well test the stoutest heart. The devoted band counted less than a hundred men,—wearied to the extreme by continued travel, with little intermission for sixty hours, over unfrequented roads and through forests, scantily and ill fed, drenched with heavy and repeated rain, chilled by cold and beating winds, in the midst of a hostile and vindictive population, away from all help, and dispirited by failure. But their indomitable leader

* Mr. Hogan's account.

still rose superior to all the difficulties that encompassed him, as well as to his own bodily infirmities. As usual, he rode in the front: *that* had always been his post, and so it was to remain to the last breath of life.

The sun had not risen far above the horizon when the advance reached the banks of the swollen and rapid Pamunkey. With celerity the men dismounted, crowded into the ferry-boat with their horses, and pushed across.

Having thus reached the farther bank, a halt was ordered, to feed the jaded horses and their riders. The scanty fare was eagerly devoured, and as much time given to rest as the circumstances permitted, after which the party once more took to the saddle. The route lay along the river-bank for three or four miles, and then away to the left for the main road.

Presently a rebel soldier started from some hiding-place, not, however, without discharging his piece at our men, which provoked a return that was fatal to him.

As the little command proceeds, and the day advances, the severity of the weather relaxes; the sun has passed the meridian, and is more than an hour on the descent, when the Mattapony is reached.

Meanwhile, the country is up and gathering about the way of the devoted band; every step of its march has been dogged.

No evidence of this appears at the ferry, which is now at hand, but still the ordinary precautions are observed, of posting a few vedettes to hold the bank while the men descend, and are ferried over in squads as numerous as the scow permits. The horses must swim.

Presently comes the crack of a rifle, then another and another ; the enemy is evidently on the track. Our vedettes unsling their carbines and return the fire, until the main force is safely over the river ; then, at the word, the rear-guard dashes down the bank, and are soon in safety with their comrades.

Colonel Dahlgren had dismounted, and placed himself by the river-side, watching and directing the passage of his men. In vain was he importuned to cross the river. He remained there, resting on his crutches, until every man and horse had passed over. When this was accomplished, he stood alone and erect, disregarding the bullets which struck near him on all sides, and calmly awaiting the return of the ferry-boat. It must have been as plain to the rebels that he, whom they made the target for their rifles, was crippled—for he needed the support of crutches—as it was that the river rolled between him and his men, separating him from all assistance. Any resolute man of their number could have rushed forward and borne away, by main force, the enfeebled frame of the young soldier. In contempt of such miserable pusillanimity, Ulric Dahlgren turned occasionally towards the bushes that sheltered these *brave* men and fired his revolver defiantly, calling on them to come out from their hiding-place.

But the gallant youth was not yet to close his glorious career; the ferry-boat bore him over unharmed, and he was once more in the saddle, riding forward with his little party.

This was about two o'clock in the afternoon, and the road they pursued led them through the woods.

It is stated that about this time the rebels took the opportunity of ascertaining exactly the number of this small force, and thus made sure that it was less than one hundred men; so they contrived to collect various scattered parties from the neighborhood, until three or four times the force of our retreating cavalry was obtained.

Even with this superiority, no effort was made to face Ulric Dahlgren and his handful of troopers, so as to bring about a fair, manly conflict in open day. Some of those who gathered about their prey had met him in Fredericksburg, and, though in far greater numbers, had been driven before him through the streets, until they fled ignominiously out of the town, and were beyond pursuit; they had no taste *now* for a repetition. So they fired from the bushes at our passing men, and hung on the rear; to relieve which Colonel Dahlgren assigned a small party to Mr. Hogan, who, for some time, performed this duty handsomely, losing but one of his men,—a result which he attributes mainly to the good conduct of his followers, conspicuous among whom was a sergeant named Scholefield.

This lasted until dark, when a bridge was reached and crossed; half a mile farther on, Colonel Dahlgren ordered a halt, in order to feed and rest his exhausted party.

The colored attendant drew a few rails from the fence near by, and spread a blanket over them; upon this rude couch the noble young soldier took his last repose. In a brief half-hour he was again awake, and once more put his men in motion.

The night was obscure, but it did not rain, and the road led chiefly among wooded land. No molestation seems to have been experienced until the final catastrophe.

With the abundant precaution that marked the whole conduct of the pursuit, an ambush had been prepared a few miles farther.

Ulric Dahlgren was, as usual, riding with the leading files. It was about midnight, and the darkness lent additional obscurity to the growth of bushes and trees through which the road lay. It is impossible to describe with accuracy the rapid succession of events that were crowded into the minute. Some rustling of leaves or branches gave token, to the keen senses of the leader, of a skulking foe. Instantly his weapon was in his hand. Words passed, but what they were, or by whom uttered, no one can say with precision,—doubtless they were not more than a peremptory challenge and reply; then came the sharp rattling volley, startling the echoes of the forest and lighting up its deepest recesses.

In that sad moment fell the horse and his heroic rider. Ulric Dahlgren was no more. Never again should he lift in defense of his country that hand, which he had raised on a sick-bed in solemn fealty to the Union cause.

All was now confusion in the ranks of that exhausted little band. The men dispersed or surrendered without resistance, and with few exceptions became captives.

It is certain now, that not a single ball struck the gallant boy in front. Four entered the left side and back, exhibiting in the most marked manner the respect felt for his martial virtues by the horde who, aided by some of that cavalry which fled in abject fear before him at Fredericksburg, sought the shelter of a midnight ambush to do their cowardly work.

Thus perished Colonel Ulric Dahlgren, before he had completed the twenty-first year of his age. He fell, as became a good soldier, at the head of his men, as a patriot and a lover of humanity; for his heart was filled with sorrow at the wretchedness of his captive comrades, and his mission was to rescue them from the cruel dungeons in which they were wasting away.

That he fell not in battle was the choice of the infamous crew that dogged his steps with greater numbers, and dared not assail him by the light of day; whose lasting shame it will be, that they made an ambush sure, by resorting to the darkest hour of night.

To the fantastic vagaries of the code that affected the borrowed plumes of a past age, he subscribed not; but as a true son of the North, a fair type of her noble youth, he followed those maxims which taught him to "*love mercy, deal justly, and walk humbly with his God.*"

To the foe, even though he confronted him as a traitor, and a bitter enemy to the Union, he always offered fair, open battle, such as one brave man might offer to another. To strike him down by the midnight bullet from the lonely ambush, as he fell himself, had no place in the rule by which he was guided. And history will not fail to write down such an act as *assassination.*

"Almost alone, without the trump and blazonry of war,
In darkness, hand to hand with death, thou wert death's conqueror."

CHAPTER XII.

"THE BEAUTY OF ISRAEL IS SLAIN UPON THY HIGH PLACES."

EVERY sentiment of civilization limits war and its dread scourges to the grave. Beyond its solemn confines human vengeance may not venture to pursue; to do otherwise is to violate every precept, Christian and humane.

Heathen moralists go even further, and proscribe ill speaking of the dead: "*de mortuis nihil nisi bonum.*" Shall the milder virtues of the gospel inculcate less?

But to insult the dead, and offer indignity to the remains of the bitterest foe, will be tolerated nowhere by the common feeling; it can only be the work of cowardly ruffians, in defiance alike of decency and law. Savages may glut their hate and fear upon a fallen or expiring enemy, but that alone is accepted everywhere as the best evidence of their brutish nature and low degree in the human family.

The ferocity which so often stained the slavery cause was in no instance more disgracefully exhibited than in the treatment to which the remains of Ulric Dahlgren were subjected.

His fall had been the signal for the surrender or dispersion of the little party that remained with him. Some betook themselves to the first friendly covert, while the greater part, hopeless of escape, collected in a field near by, and there awaited the captivity that seemed inevitable.

Here it would be supposed the bitterest hate might pause and be sated. Not so. What ensued was well in accord with the atrocity that doomed captives to worse than death.

The light of the following morning fell on a spectacle that might have shamed the most ferocious nature that ever disgraced humanity. Upon the bare ground, near the roadside, was stretched the lifeless body of Ulric Dahlgren; not as he fell, but stripped of every vestige of garment. The absent limb told of battle, and proud achievement, and patriotic sacrifice; the severed finger was the work of the midnight thief.

The villainous act was not perpetrated by the wretched creatures who follow the camp, and flit like vultures about the battle-field, but by the men of the surrounding country, in arms for *their* cause; "*the farmers by day, and the felons by night*," so indignantly denounced by the preacher in his tribute to the heroic dead.

Truly, such was a fitting consummation of the

midnight ambush and the dishonest blow of the assassin's bullet.

Presently came the sad train of captive Union soldiers, on their way to the very dungeons from which they had hoped to release their comrades. It is said that they were marched by the spot where, thus inhumanly exposed, lay the body of their noble young leader, all insensible to the outrage.

Be it remembered that these infamous acts were committed before the rebel authorities had thought fit to fashion the objects of the expedition after their own views; they were done with unheated blood, and merely followed the instincts of the perpetrators.

After the news had reached Richmond that Colonel Dahlgren had fallen, and that the handful of men with him had been dispersed or captured, it was bruited about that the purpose of the expedition was *solely* to destroy Richmond, and to slay the chiefs of the rebellion,—a statement well calculated to inflame the population, not yet recovered from the abject dread into which they had been thrown by the appearance of the Union cavalry so near the city, and justly apprehensive of the consequences that might ensue from the sudden release of the Union soldiers immured in the cells of Libby and Belle Isle: *to* them no mercy had been shown, what, therefore, could be expected *from* them?

A mob is proverbially cruel and cowardly; nothing, therefore, was so likely to work upon their passions as such a rumor. The publication of orders asserted to have been found on the person of Colonel Dahlgren followed in a few days, and on Monday the body of the gallant youth was disinterred, and brought to Richmond, where it was exposed to public view, at the depot of the York River Railroad.

Nothing better was permitted to the precious remains than a common pine box, the coarse shirt and pantaloons of a rebel soldier, with an ordinary camp-blanket for a shroud.

The once perfect proportions had been sadly mutilated. The limb that was gone suggested remembrance of an event most abhorrent to rebeldom, —when at Gettysburg its best army recoiled before the men of the Union, and Ulric Dahlgren, leading a desperate charge into Hagerstown, hesitated not to peril his life in an effort to destroy the trains of the retreating host. The missing finger told another story, one of utter and infamous turpitude. It had borne a ring,—a plain gold ring,—of little worth if counted in mere dross, but inestimable as the memorial of a dearly-loved, deceased sister. To secure this, the assassins who waylaid his steps and did midnight murder from the shelter of a hedge, hesitated not to violate the sanctity of death, and mutilate the noble hand which had so often been raised against their armed treason, in behalf of his bleeding country; it was a deed truly in keeping with the events that went before and followed.

Were there none in that crowd who looked with loathing upon the spectacle, and were touched at the sight of his extreme youth, and felt how utterly fiendish and cowardly it was, thus to desecrate the dead?

The mob gazed, no doubt, as mobs always do, with exultation that their fear was at an end. They little dreamed that the avenger was not far off, that, before the year had expired, their unholy rebellion would be withering, as a scroll, before the blazing banner of the republic, Grant at the very portals of Richmond, and Sherman looming up from the south, like a rising storm, branding in terrible characters the doom of treason. Their very city would be consuming with desolating fires, kindled, not by the hands of Union soldiers, but by the orders of their own authorities. They saw not the writing on the wall, but yet *it was before them.*

So there lay the maimed but noble relics of the Union martyr, entirely heedless of all that the hate and fear of his enemies could bestow: the ignominy was theirs.

When the gaze of the tiger-horde had been sated, the body disappeared from public view; it was doomed to concealment in some nameless spot. How vain!

It was to justify these ruthless acts that the announcement, already mentioned, had been spread about in regard to *the orders* alleged to have been found on Colonel Dahlgren after he fell, which were said to have directed the death of the insurgent President and the destruction of Richmond.

But the unrighteous purpose of the rebel authorities was defeated in the fullness of time, and the remains of Ulric Dahlgren, which had been so brutally insulted in Richmond, were received with every mark of respect and sorrow in the capital of the nation and in the principal cities of the two States through which they passed. In Washington, they reposed in the Council-chamber of the city, and, after an eloquent discourse by one of our most eminent divines, which was listened to by the President, several members of the Cabinet, and a throng of sympathizing citizens, they were conveyed, through Baltimore, to Philadelphia, were laid in the time-honored Hall of Independence, where another touching address was delivered, and were then attended to the grave with every military honor.

And thus, as always, violence and injustice fell short of the aim intended; nay, more, they recoiled on their perpetrators in the end with tenfold more effect than upon the object of their ferocious and unrelenting hate. The barbarity of the proceedings just mentioned operated to the detriment of the cause that it was designed to serve, for it proved by deed more conclusively than could be done by words that the rebellion disgraced the most sacred instincts of humanity in waging war against the lawful government. It showed to the whole world that the spirit that animated it was utterly at variance with every principle of civilized life. The evils of war have too often been aggravated by disgraceful excesses, but never under the avowed sanction of high authority, and they seldom admit of extenuation, except under the plea of hot blood and sanguinary battle. Here, with calm pulse, and with deliberate design, we have a set of men assuming to be a government, giving their sanction, if not direction, to the most heartless and disgraceful desecration of a dead body. It justified the avenging sword which, they alleged, had been leveled at their own lives, and invoked a retribution, without appeal, on their own heads, unless, indeed, it could have been urged as an exception to their general conduct of the war, as a solitary departure from a kind and merciful treatment of those whom the fortune of battle had made their prisoners. *Was this so?* Far from it. It was only one more dark spot on the blood-stained blazonry of disloyal war; the very object to which Ulric Dahlgren had devoted his life was the rescue of his comrades from a captivity unparalleled in horrors. Thousands of our men were perishing, by slow and cruel death, in the dungeons of Richmond,—by hunger and thirst, by the heat of summer and the chill of winter, by slow, wasting disease, and filth, and vermin, or, at times, by a welcome bullet from the jailer-guard. In this association come the memory of Fort Pillow, and the massacre of our unresisting soldiers; the incarceration of fifty Union officers, at Charleston, placed where our artillery fire was heaviest,—the purpose not to be mistaken or disavowed, for it was officially notified; the pursuit of escaping prisoners by bloodhounds; the disinterment, at Charleston, of the body of an officer* of the Union fleet, who had been mortally wounded on the ruined walls of Sumter, while gallantly leading his men to the assault. There was no pretext to justify the least slight to this brave officer; and yet, when, by the pious care of a friendly hand,† his mortal remains had been consigned to the grave, they were not permitted to rest there undisturbed, but were rudely dragged thence, and ejected from Magnolia Cemetery, as if the dust of the Union soldier were not worthy to mingle with the best of the land.‡

* Lieutenant Bradford, United States marines, September, 1863.

† Dr. Mackey, of Charleston.

‡ March 16, 1865. Admiral Dahlgren caused the remains of this brave man to be transferred from the potters' field, and interred, with military honors and Christian rites, in the finest site of Magnolia Cemetery.

Such a catalogue was fitly concluded with the murder of our beloved President, not in the fray of the field by the sword of the soldier, but by the bullet of a base assassin, who, stealing upon the hour of innocent recreation, took a noble life from the country, and, in the exultant utterance of the instant thought, fully proclaimed to what counsels he owed his inspiration. Nor was it intended that the design should be limited to this great sacrifice. Another, high in state, had been marked, but the hand of the sneaking wretch who stole into the sick-chamber of his victim failed him at the moment when he would have taken life.

Such was the bitter and remorseless spirit that unholy rebellion called to its aid, and which spread over its confines, until it became the practice, if not the principle, of disloyalty.

What right had those who invoked it, to cry out against the just consequences of their own ruthless system, or to ask for mercy when the chief conspirators were in the hands of justice, to answer for the treason which has blighted this fair land with all the horrors of civil war, and brought death and desolation to so many hearth-stones? Why did they not proclaim the rule of action *then*, as *now*, to be, that

"*There is a time in the affairs of men when narrow-minded prejudice and vituperation should cease. It is only the bloodhound that will hunt his victim down,*

THE TRUE SIGNATURE.

Ulric Dahlgren

THE FORGED SIGNATURE.

U. Dahlgren
Col Comd

as it were, to the very tomb, and there bay at the dead victim."*

Why should this sentiment, so true under all circumstances, have been discarded from the memory of rebeldom, until the lives of its leaders had been brought into jeopardy, and they were arraigned at the bar of justice?

But, as often happens when bad passions control action, the conduct of the rebel authorities was not excused even by the plea which they set up as sufficient. The document alleged to have been found upon the person of Colonel Dahlgren is utterly discredited by the fact that the signature attached to it cannot possibly be his own, because it is not his name,—a letter is misplaced, and the real name *Dahlgren* is spelled *Dalhgren;* hence it is undeniable that the paper is not only spurious, but is a forgery. Evidence, almost as positive, is to be found in the writing of the Christian prefix of the signature. The document is signed "*U.* Dalhgren," whereas Colonel Dahlgren invariably signed himself "*Ulric* Dahlgren," *never with the bare initial of the first name.* Among all the letters of his writing which can be collected, not an instance to the contrary occurs, down to the last that he ever wrote, just before starting for Richmond.

---

* Columbus Times.

It is entirely certain that no such orders were ever *issued* by Colonel Dahlgren. All that he gave were verbal, as might have been expected under the circumstances, and in no case intimated, in the least degree, the intention conveyed by the obnoxious passages of the spurious order. Nothing of the kind was received by the officers or privates of the command, even to the time when Richmond was in view; and it is highly improbable that they would have been uninformed of any important purpose of the expedition when they were supposed to be on the verge of action. Lieutenant Bartley, the signal-officer of the column, in a published letter,* after giving an account of the treatment received when a prisoner, says:

"All this brutal punishment was inflicted upon us, according to the statement of the Confederate prison officials, on account of those papers said to have been found on the body of Colonel Dahlgren at the time he was killed. But the name of Colonel Dahlgren can never be injured by any slander or forgery that can be concocted by all the enemies of our country. His deeds speak for themselves. His career with Sigel, Burnside, Hooker, Meade, and Kilpatrick, together with his exploits at Fredericksburg, Beverley Ford, Chambersburg, and in front

* December 29, 1864.

of Richmond, will live when the name of the last traitor in the land is forgotten.

"I pronounce those papers a *base forgery*, and will give some of my reasons for so doing. I was with the expedition in the capacity of signal-officer, and was the only staff-officer with him. I had charge of all the material for destroying bridges, blowing up locks, aqueducts, etc. I knew all his plans, what he intended to do and how he intended doing it, and I know that I never received any such instructions as those papers are said to contain. I also heard all the orders and instructions given to the balance of the officers of the command. Men cannot carry out orders they know nothing of. The colonel's instructions were, that if we were successful in entering the city, to *take no life except in combat;* to keep all prisoners safely guarded, but to *treat them with respect;* liberate all the Union prisoners, destroy the public buildings and government stores, and leave the city by way of the Peninsula."

It is, of course, entirely superfluous to analyze a document as to chirography, or other details, so long as the signature is an unquestioned forgery, for that determines all; and, failing as a vindication, it becomes an aggravation of the infamous treatment inflicted upon the remains of a true and undaunted son of the country.

The expedition to Richmond was undertaken

solely to release the captive Union soldiers, who were penned by thousands in its wretched prisons, suffering and dying from want of food and the most ordinary necessaries of life. *But for that object*, it would never have been thought of.

The orders of Colonel Dahlgren to his column were in accordance with this purpose: the prisons were also to be destroyed, and all public property, and stores of a military character. If prisoners were taken, they were to be well guarded, but not ill treated, and no life was to be taken except in conflict.

It is certain, from the testimony of a competent living witness, that such were the orders, and the *only* orders, given to him by Colonel Dahlgren, or that he heard given to others; and as the duties of this officer were confidential, and kept him near the colonel until his death, his evidence is conclusive in the matter.

It is not to be supposed that the execution of the project would be unattended with more or less danger to the lives and property of the people and their families.

The prisons in which our men were huddled had been located within the limits of the city, and to burst open the doors of their dungeons would have been to strike but the *first* blow for their liberty; for, though numbering thousands, they were unarmed in the midst of the best army of rebeldom, and far away from the nearest Union lines. It was but reasonable to suppose that instant and persistent efforts would be made to recapture them, regardless of the destruction that might ensue; and it was certain that our men, already driven to desperation by the most iniquitous treatment, would resist to the death, rather than return to the horrid dungeons from which they had just escaped.

The character of such a struggle can hardly be conceived. What the rebel authorities had determined upon in such a contingency, was well understood to be the instant and wholesale extermination of all these captives,—blowing up them and their prisons by mines placed for the purpose. It is hard to imagine that the intent to commit such a massacre would be admitted, but the committee of the rebel Congress had the hardihood to avow and to justify it:

"Your committee proceed next to notice the allegation, that the Confederate authorities had prepared a mine under the Libby Prison, and placed in it a quantity of gunpowder, for the purpose of blowing up the buildings with their inmates, in case of an attempt to rescue them.

"A mine was prepared under the Libby Prison, a sufficient quantity of gunpowder was put into it, and pains was taken to inform the prisoners that any attempt at escape made by them would be effectually defeated. The plan succeeded perfectly.

The prisoners were awed and kept quiet. Dahlgren and his party were defeated and scattered," etc.*

Who shall be held answerable for such atrocity,—the comrades of these unfortunate men, who only sought to rescue them, or they who, violating every instinct of humanity and the law by which war seeks to restrain its own terrors, degraded the high place of their power into a city of dungeons, and there accumulated upon their prisoners horrors equaled only by the protracted agonies of the stake?

Even if the treatment of our men had been in all respects conformable to usage, there was no necessity for placing them in the midst of a city, where their liberation might be effected by our military operations at any time, and subject unarmed people and their property to danger.

The Union government only performed a bounden duty when it took measures to release its soldiers from such a captivity, irrespective of all consequences to those whose misfortune or fault it was to be near. The flames which would have consumed those infamous dungeons might have extended to the neighboring dwellings; but would they have been as destructive as the explosion of the mines that was to send thousands of the captive soldiers to their last account at a single blow? Doubtless, too, in the hot haste of the fray, it would have been

---

* Washington Evening Star, March 31, 1865.

impossible for our men to strike just where they should, at the moment when every effort was being made to destroy them, or to return them to prison.

The guilt of these deplorable consequences, as well as of the original offense, would have belonged to the rebel authorities who ordered or tolerated such enormities.

How far they were sincere in the indignation which they professed, at the possible results to the city of an attempt to rescue the prisoners, may be judged from the unhesitating application of the torch, by their orders (when our troops were about to enter, a year later), to some paltry stores which they wished to prevent falling into our hands.

The historian thus tells the tale:*

"At the same time the Union force on the lines confronting Richmond from the north side of the James was startled by a clamorous uproar, and the sky was seen to be lit up with a lurid glare.

"But the Confederate officials, in addition to this work of destruction† (which cannot be condemned on the score that it was not warranted by the rules of war), adopted a measure shocking to every sense of humanity. It appears that the warehouses of Richmond contained great store of government tobacco, and the cruel and senseless order was

---

* Swinton, 607.

† The blowing up of their iron-clads.

given to fire these, as though it were possible with impunity to play with the devouring element; the flames spreading to the neighboring buildings soon involved a wide and widening area; and, though the Union force on its entry labored to put out the fire, it could not be subdued until the heart of the city, including all the business section, was laid in ashes. It was amid such scenes that Richmond fell, with the smoke of the torment of the Confederacy ascending to heaven, while, far away, all that remained of the Confederate army hastened beyond the sunset."

The mischief did not stop here, but, as if retributive justice designed that the last blow at the rebellion should come from its own leaders, it extended further, and trod out the last hope of the able leader of their armies.

According to the historian,*

"When Lee determined to abandon Petersburg and Richmond, he dispatched orders that large supplies of commissary and quartermaster's stores should be sent forward from Danville to Amelia Court House, there to await the arrival of his columns. When, however, on Sunday afternoon, the loaded train of cars reached Amelia Court House, the officer in charge was met by an order from the Richmond authorities to bring on the

* Swinton, 608.

train to Richmond, it being the design to use the cars in the transportation of the personal and other property of the Confederate government. Interpreting this order in the sense that the train and its contents should be taken to Richmond, the officer, without unloading the stores at Amelia Court House, carried on cars, freight and all; and the rations on which Lee had depended for the subsistence of his army were consumed in the general conflagration of Richmond.

"Such were the agonizing tidings that met the Confederate commander on his arrival at Amelia Court House, and one can well imagine how, from that moment, all his hopes were dashed to the ground."

A few days afterwards, Lee surrendered.

But besides the dangers to which the rebel authorities had exposed Richmond, by placing the prisons within its precincts, they had invited to it the most strenuous efforts of our military operations, by divesting it entirely of the character of a peaceful city, and making it the very center of their power, political and military. Here was their general government itself, with all its machinery, executive and legislative, the grand army upon which rested their every hope, with the immense supplies required for its support, and the principal cannon foundry, from which issued the ordnance that lined the parapets of the works scattered over the Southern country.

Richmond was at once a capital, a camp, and an arsenal, the heart and the bulwark of the rebellion; upon the possession of which depended its existence. Towards it had been urged the steps of our main army, in every campaign, for four years,—from the beginning to the end,—under McDowell, McClellan, Burnside, Hooker, Meade, and Grant. While Richmond stood, the rebellion was erect; and its last hope was not extinguished until the flag of the Union waved over that stronghold.

For these reasons the citizens and their families should have been removed from the place; for so long as they remained there they were unavoidably exposed to the same perils as the armed force that defended the city. The roads were entirely open to them at all times; their presence could not be permitted to ward off the blow of war in any shape, —if they *would* remain, the blame and the consequences descended on them. They did remain, and did suffer, but not at the hands of Union soldiers; their own authorities gave Richmond to the flames.

As to the personal risk to which the leaders of the rebellion might be liable, in the event of our cavalry having been able to effect an entrance into Richmond and liberate the Union soldiers, it is not to be considered for a moment.

By the ordinary rules of war, they were not exempt from any danger to which the meanest soldier who followed them was exposed. It would be puerile to enter upon an argument to establish this, for, by the first principle on which war proceeds, all engaged in battle are liable to be slain, so long as resistance is continued; and it was worse than puerile for the head of the rebellion and his counselors, guarded by an army of one hundred thousand men, to denounce attempts to slay or capture them as public enemies by a handful of daring men.

The purpose of Ulric Dahlgren had a far more exalted aim than their death or capture; and yet, even if the object of the enterprise had been to attack the leaders in the very stronghold of their power, it would have been in accordance with the rules of war.

History tells us that when the Spartan king found he could no longer defend the mountain-pass, where he had placed himself to stay the march of the Persian host, he took advantage of the night to enter the camp of the enemy at the head of a chosen band of six hundred men, intending to kill the king; he perished in the attempt, with all his men, and his dead body was visited with every indignity by an affrighted and cruel enemy, on the ground that such purpose was not justified by the rules of war.

It no doubt suited the rebel leaders to invest their persons with an additional safeguard, by bringing reproach on the daring gallantry of their antagonist; but the distinguished jurist Vattel, acknowledged as high authority by all nations, takes very different ground upon the question. He says of these Spartans, "Their expedition was according to the common rules of war. And the king could not treat them more rigorously than other enemies. A strict watch baffles such irruption," etc. (Page 534.)

Colonel Dahlgren and his five hundred would, therefore, have been justified by the laws of war in slaying the rebel leaders in their camp, just as the Spartan king and his six hundred *have been justified* in their effort to slay the Persian monarch. And why should they shrink from the dangers of their position more than from its honors? Where is the place of a leader, if not in the foremost ranks? It was there, at the head of his men, that the bullets of the midnight ambush found Ulric Dahlgren, and where he had placed himself fully prepared to abide whatever fate the perils of the conflict might bring. The last words ever penned by his noble hand recognized the dangers of the undertaking, without moving his resolution to face them. He declared there was *no better place to die.* And, doubtless, the same sentiment animated his gallant heart up to the moment when it ceased to throb forever.

What a contrast to the pitiful cry raised by the high ones of rebeldom, at the bare idea of risk to their own precious persons!

Would it not have been immeasurably better for the insurgent chief himself to have struck a manly blow in his own defense, and have died by the sabers of our Union soldiers, rather than to close his career, flying ignobly from the horrible Golgotha where he had reigned so long, proclaimed as a felon, with a price on his head, and finally to have been captured as he was?

Was he less a felon in March, 1864, when our little band appeared before his citadel, than afterwards when in his cell, and liable to answer with life for his share in the rebellion?

If, then, the leaders of a hostile force, engaged in rightful war, could plead no immunity from bullet or bayonet more than their humblest followers, and no security from being surprised and slain in their camps save the vigilance of a sufficient guard, by what standard shall be measured the privileges of the heads of a rebellion under similar circumstances?

The United States conducted the war for the suppression of the insurrection according to the customary rules, from a regard to what was merely humane; but this was no more than a temporary concession,—the postponement of a right to inflict condign punishment, according to the responsibilities of the several actors, to be resumed whenever circumstances should permit due enforcement.

Well might those who stood in the front of the

rebellion ponder, often and seriously, upon the heavy accountability they had incurred by instigating and precipitating this terrible civil war. Never had such an extreme resort been less justified by the acts or intentions of the existing government, or by the objects which the insurrection proposed to effect by dissolving the Union.

Under its banner the States had attained a measure of prosperity, and enjoyed a degree of freedom, unexampled in all the previous history of mankind. The South not only shared fully in these results, but, by reason of influences due to its peculiar institution, possessed a controlling power in the general government. To the date of secession, the several Presidents had been either from the South, or opposed to any proposition likely to affect slavery. The voice of abolition was scarcely heard in Congress, and was unrepresented in the judiciary, or any branch of the executive. Though the new President was opposed to the principles of slavery, he was equally adverse to any interference with the guarantees of the Constitution, and, at all events, would have been controlled by the majority in Congress, which, with the judiciary, was unchanged in its views of slavery. These important facts had been impressed fully on the South by some few of their prominent men (and particularly by Mr. A. H. Stephens), who were not yet absolutely insane with passion or apprehension.

But it was in vain to attempt to stay the madness of the hour. The only remedy it looked to was secession, which, in principle, was essentially equivalent to severing not only the bond of the National Union, but of all political union whatever. Once admitted, State might *secede* from State, and county from county, until society was resolved into the original elements of individual strength and force. It meant political chaos, civil war, foreign intervention, perhaps even foreign domination. Before its baneful influence would fade the great Western star of equal rights, under whose benignant rays was rising the greatest empire of self-government that the world had ever seen. In a word, SECESSION was division and misrule, national suicide, and, if once entered upon, could only be restrained by despotic power.

By the rebellion, slavery, with the lash and the fetter, was to be perpetuated,—curse alike to master and man; it was the greatest crime against humanity enforced by war, the greatest crime against civilization, and, as such, had not the least claim to countenance from any law, or sympathy from living being.

The purpose of *secession* was not only to pull down the best and set up the worst form of government, but that purpose was carried out with every species of aggravation and insult. The forts, arsenals, navy yards, post-offices, and treasure of the United States were seized without scruple, while the government looked on as meekly as if it acquiesced,—President Buchanan declaring that he had no right to resort to coercion. As if determined to degrade as well as to destroy, Sumter was attacked and captured.

Only then did the lawful government begin to enforce its just authority, but to the least possible extent. President Lincoln summoned troops, not to *coerce* the seceding States, but solely to recover the United States property that had been seized. That moderate measure was sufficient, however, to disclose the desperate and uncompromising purposes, as well as the stupendous preparation, of the rebellion. The leaders appealed to the sword for decision, and by nothing else would they abide.

Having thus, without reason or pretext, defied lawful authority and initiated war, as if to close the door to the least effort at reconciliation, the leaders prosecuted their resistance with a ferocity and contempt of the laws of war which has no parallel. Sometimes our men were butchered after surrender, as at Fort Pillow; prisoners were penned by thousands, until they melted away faster than on the battle-field; and Libby, Andersonville, and other places became infamous. If they escaped from such cruelty, the bloodhound was loosed on their track. Our officers were purposely confined under the fire of our own guns, and the body of one, who had been mortally wounded in battle, was dug up and cast from the cemetery where it had been interred. Mines were placed under the prisons of Richmond, by which unarmed captives were to be hurled into eternity by thousands in an instant.

Finally, when no hope of success remained, the leaders madly rejected all offers of accommodation, and prolonged the contest until every resource which they could command was exhausted, and until fire and sword had devastated their country,—themselves kindling the flames which laid in ashes most of their own capital.

Thus treason was followed by ferocious violation of the rules of war, and by outraging every instinct of humanity, until woe and death rested, like a pall, over the *whole* land.

Who can deny to the perpetration of such enormities the verdict of the ordinary law, thus defined by high authority?—

"All the right of a power to make war is derived from the justice of his cause. Whoever, therefore, takes arms without a lawful cause, can absolutely have no kind of right; all the hostilities he commits are unjust.

"He is chargeable with all the evils, all the horrors, of the war; all the effusion of blood, the desolation of families, the rapine, the violences, the ravages, the burnings, are his works and his crimes. He is guilty towards the enemy of attacking, oppressing, massacring them without cause; guilty towards his people of drawing them into acts of injustice, exposing their lives without necessity, without reason. Lastly, he is guilty towards all mankind of disturbing their quiet and setting a pernicious example. Shocking catalogue of miseries and crimes!" (Vattel, 561.)

Well might the instigators and leaders of the rebellion quail before such an accountability; they had taken their lives in their hands when they appealed to the sword, and by that decision must abide. And yet, at the first glimpse of danger near their own high place, their outcry rang far and wide. Though encompassed by all their power, they betrayed the agony of their fear by savagely spurning the gallant dead.

And what reproach could justly be laid upon the famished and maddened captives of Libby when they sallied from its cells and met their oppressors,—eager to slay or to fetter them again,—if they smote right and left regardless of all but escape?

The laws of war are for those who regard them.

The fair fame of the youthful soldier cannot be dimmed by aught that his inhuman butchers can urge, more than the frail tenement, which his noble spirit once animated, could feel the indignities which they visited upon it. The horrors which surrounded his fall will not be forgotten, and will always disgrace alike the perpetrators and those who sanctioned such atrocity. The midnight ambush of the abject villains, who feared to face him and his exhausted followers in open day, the pillage of the dead body, even to the last thread that decency demanded,—mere low theft, such as a street-burglar would blush at,—the savage and wanton mutilation of the hand, in order to secure a small ring, the forgery, the desecration of the grave, and the exposure of the body to the gaze of a mob, the attempt to conceal it in a nameless grave, all betray the instincts of violent and brutish natures; and were appropriately followed by efforts of the murderers to obtain the price of blood from the parent of their victim, by offering for sale some of the articles which they had so shamefully stolen from a dead body.

Contrast the high and holy purpose of the Union soldier, his devotion to it, even to death; his calm, undaunted courage, graced by every milder virtue; his kind hospitality to the captive rebel officers; contrast these with the craven cowardice of the ruffians who beset him, their brutal treatment of his body, and, worse than these, the crimes of the higher so-called chivalry, who made war on the dead as only such could wage, and say if it were not happier to die, as did Ulric Dahlgren, so true, so gentle, and so brave, than to live, as do those who, having outraged his grave and his name, now stand before the law, suitors for mercy?

By loyal men and by the friends of freedom and humanity, Ulric Dahlgren will be remembered, as a faithful and fearless champion of right and of his country, and as a victim to his sympathy for oppressed captives, to rescue whom he put aside all thought for life, liberty, and name.

That he ever intended to add one pang to the inevitable evils that might attend such an enterprise is not borne out by any evidence, and is contradicted by the false signature, and by the tenor of a whole life.

On the other hand, they who ruthlessly held our captive soldiers in savage bonds, and in cold blood destined them to a sudden and common death if they attempted to escape, justified by such iniquitous deeds any penalty that might befall them.

Ulric Dahlgren was twenty-one years and eleven months of age when he closed his bright career.

He was tall and graceful in movement; his well-knit frame gave promise of more than usual strength, but lacked the development of matured manhood, and was divested of all spare flesh by a life of constant exertion.

His mind was of no common order, and had been carefully trained. He was well read in the classics, a good mathematician, and expert with the pencil.

Having passed so much leisure in the naval ordnance department, he had a rare knowledge of artillery and its use, which he often turned to good account * on the field of battle.

He delighted in all manly exercises, was perfectly at ease in the water, and, as a horseman, was unsurpassed,—a bold, practiced, and elegant rider.

In action, his discernment of objects and conception were almost instant; in judgment deliberate, but in execution rapid as lightning, with which he united courage so clear and unshaken as to permit his faculties the most undisturbed exercise under any circumstances. He never seemed to be conscious of the least danger to himself, and the only visible effect on him of its presence were the slightly-compressed lip and the sparkle of the eye. His personal bearing, at such a time, is well described by Captain Mitchell, who speaks of him, and of the impression the colonel made upon him, when he rode along the front of his column, then near Richmond, under a heavy fire and about to charge the enemy's infantry.

To the casual observer he appeared like a very young and rather diffident man, gentle and unobtrusive, a moderate talker, and always of pleasant mood. But beneath, lay a character of the firmest

---

* General Sigel says, "I gave him charge of the ordnance department, which duties he fulfilled with great energy and ability."

mould, a constancy of purpose never to be diverted from its object, intrepidity not to be disturbed by any emergency, impulses of the purest nature habitually in exercise, all producing a course of life unblemished by the least meanness. Loyal to every obligation, he was, therefore, a good son, and never failed in the most respectful obedience to his parent. A warm and sincere friend, he was true through good and ill report; devoted to the honored cause of his country, he never heeded toil or danger where his service was needed.

To these qualities he added a deep sense of religious obligation, chiefly due to the precepts and example of his departed mother; but in this, as in other respects, he was not demonstrative. When lying wounded, and seemingly near the verge of death, he was reminded of the danger which he did not appear to be aware of. Smiling feebly, he replied that he knew it, and added that he had never gone into battle without asking forgiveness for his sins and commending his soul to his Maker.

Such was the even tenor of his life, not flashing out at intervals, but giving forth its steady light without intermission through all its brief term.

The stamp of official recognition is thus declared by high authority:

"WASHINGTON, July 24, 1863.

"DEAR SIR,—Inclosed you have a commission for colonel, without having passed through the intermediate grade of major. Your gallant and meritorious service has, I think, entitled you to this distinction, although it is a departure from general usage which is only justified by distinguished merit such as yours. I hope you may speedily recover, and it will rejoice me to be the instrument of your further advancement in the service.

"With great respect, I am yours truly,

"EDWIN M. STANTON.

"COLONEL ULRIC DAHLGREN."

General Sigel, with whom he served for a year, writes thus:

"I cannot in this short memorandum do him justice, but will always remember him as one of the most noble, most faithful, and most valorous soldiers of the republic; as one who was equally '*excelsior*' by his manly virtues as by his intelligence and ability. His premature death struck deeply into my heart, where he will be treasured forever."

The testimonials and regrets, that reached his father from every direction when his tragic end became known, showed how widely and deeply his virtues and his patriotism were appreciated.

In the perilous events that gathered about the closing hours of life, it has been seen from the extracts of a letter, by one of his officers,* how he appeared to those around him.

The thoughts that filled the heart and mind of the young chief, and his fearless view of possible results, are exhibited in the last letter to his father,† penned, no doubt, in the solitude of his tent, during the silent hours of the night, just as he was about to start upon the final enterprise of his glorious life. Almost face to face with death, his last words were, "*If we do not return, there is no better place to 'give up the ghost.'*"

One of the finest tributes ever given in any language to departed worth, thus sums up in a few words the character and aspirations of this son of a free land:

"COLONEL ULRIC DAHLGREN.

"From time to time during this war there have been deaths in battle which have gone to the hearts of loyal millions as personal griefs, and which have carried a private sorrow into many households which the martyrs had never entered. Such were the deaths of ELLSWORTH, of WINTHROP, of SHAW, each, for a different reason, claiming sympathy and regret. Such is the death of ULRIC DAHLGREN, murdered week before last on the Peninsula, after

---

* Captain Mitchell.

† Already given, page 211, chapter xi.

he had fought his way through the forces which surrounded him,—shot by a guerrilla-party in ambush, when he had a right to believe himself in safety.

"Young as he was—dying at twenty-two—his military career is crowded with events, and around his smooth brow the laurel had already clustered thickly.

"'A man that is young in years may be old in hours,' says Bacon, 'if he have lost no time; but that happeneth rarely.' Measured by such a standard, judged by what he had done, and what he was, this boy was a veteran. He was born a soldier, and his earliest service in the field found him the same cool, wary, skillful, indomitable leader which his last months of more conspicuous action showed him to the country.

"He was a man whom his men trusted, and would follow. That personal magnetism—the chemical union of extraordinary will and power of command with winning and affectionate qualities—which is the essential character of the best leaders in battle, he possessed. Napoleon said the Old Guard would follow Ney farther than they would him. The irresistible influence which belonged to Ney belonged to DAHLGREN. There was something about him which perpetually recalled to mind the historic traits and descriptive peculiarities of men famous in battle.

"The white plume of Navarre did not more

grandly shine in the front of the hottest fight, than the pale, resolute face and burning eyes of this young captain. He scarcely ever was in an action where great odds were not against him, yet never was in an action out of which he did not bring fame for himself. He was not rash, but he did numberless things which for another to attempt would have been rash. The superiority of numbers was often on the other side; the superiority of force was always on his.

"Different traits of his character need equally to be stated, before he can be rightly understood. It seems a rude act, almost, to uncover in public the diffident grace and sweetness which made the beauty of his private life. The iron hand he had, but the glove of velvet was seldom drawn off. Few men make themselves so loved as he did,—so loved, so trusted, so little envied, while winning such large honors as came to him almost unsought.

"Devoted to his profession for its own sake, bound to it still more for the sake of his country, he broke away from the dearest private ties, and yet carried with him into the field the tenderness and purity of character, which seemed inseparable from the fireside and from home.

"It is this young martyred hero whom the Richmond press, speaking for the rebel leaders, have painted as a sort of fiend; whose body they mangled after death, and whose name they have sought to disgrace with still more horrible insults.

"In passionate and cruel anger at an attack which so nearly succeeded, they have threatened to murder every prisoner taken, and apparently, in order to justify it, or to stimulate their ferocity, they have forged orders said to have been found on Colonel DAHLGREN for the murder of Jefferson Davis and his Cabinet. The prisoners in our hands, and the known purpose of our government to retaliate for the barbarous treatment of white men, will prevent the execution of rebel threats, but will not prevent them from avenging themselves on an enemy in his grave,—a trait which they possess and exhibit in common with other savage and treacherous races. It can do no harm to the memory of Colonel DAHLGREN; and if it did, we may be sure that he would cheerfully endure reproach, as in his life he endured hardship and pain, for the service of his country."*

It soothes sharp regrets to feel that, short as was the allotted term, it was sufficient to give the full character, in all its depth and beauty, so complete that years would have done no more. It is truly said that one hour may make a name and a destiny, as well as an age.

There must have been no myth, but a glowing

---

* New York Independent.

reality in such a being, to call forth from one mature in age and worthily high in a community's esteem, such a burst as this:

"The account of young Dahlgren's death reads like an ancient romance. How sad! how brilliant! how wonderful! what devotion! what intrepidity! what patriotism!

"I recalled the appearance of the pale, maimed youth, who sat on your piazza on the day of the funeral; when I pressed his hand, and he mine, as though we were blood relations, though we had never seen each other before. How he could have gained strength to ride on one of those painful, exhausting raids surpasses comprehension.

"But there he was, fighting like a hero, dying like a martyr, his body stripped and insulted, and ignominiously buried. His memory will live when we are all dead and forgotten.

"My tears drop right down while reading the extracts from the Richmond papers,—tears of sorrow, of anger, of joy that my country has produced such a noble youth, and that she has more."

Such was the brave and generous spirit whose light has been so early quenched forever. That, of itself, might have sufficed to sate the bitterest vengeance. The shocking cruelty that has been exhibited in the treatment of his inanimate body will, in the end, recoil on the infamous ruffians who perpetrated it.

To the gallant young soldier it has been as nothing, for he has passed away to his final account, leaving behind him a name far beyond the reach of his enemies. There are those left, whose pride and pleasure it will be to vindicate his fair fame, and he will be remembered as a young patriot of spotless life and purest purpose ; honest, true, and gentle, dutiful to every obligation ; unselfish and generous to a fault ; an undaunted soldier of the Union, who never struck a blow except at an armed enemy ; an accomplished gentleman, a sincere Christian, a faithful comrade, who, although not having recovered from the almost fatal illness consequent on losing a limb in battle, went forth to brave every hardship, in the hope of aiding to release our captive soldiers from the dungeons of a merciless enemy, who, for this, sought vengeance on his dead body with the ferocity of savages.

CHAPTER XIII.

CONCLUSION—RECOVERY OF THE REMAINS—FUNERAL DISCOURSES AND OBSEQUIES.

THE painful tidings of Ulric Dahlgren's fate came very slowly to Washington.

His father had arrived there from his squadron, off Charleston, on the 2d of March, little conscious that on the night of that day his beloved son was closing his mortal career near Richmond. He learned of his absence immediately on reaching home, but felt no misgivings on the subject, except as to the capability of his son to withstand the exposure of such an expedition, when his health was so far from being fully established.

About two days later, the President, with his characteristic kindness, sent a few lines on a card to Admiral Dahlgren, saying that General Kilpatrick was safe at Fortress Monroe, but that Colonel Dahlgren was missing; and the following day (Saturday, 5th) Mr. Lincoln wrote that he was said to be a prisoner.

These tidings naturally occasioned great concern in the family, which was measurably relieved on Sunday, when the President called at the residence of the admiral, to say that he had just received a telegram from General Butler, at Fortress Monroe, to the effect that Ulric was not a prisoner, but was at King-and-Queen Court House, and that he would send some troops there to bring him in.

This state of suspense did not continue long. The mournful certainty reached Washington soon after, and on Tuesday the President sent for the admiral, in order to disclose to him the death of his gallant son, tidings of which had arrived the day before. The bereaved father lost no time in leaving on board of the steamer that had brought him North, and still lay at the Navy Yard ready for sea, which, without delay, carried him to Fortress Monroe by ten o'clock next day. He there received from General Butler copies of Richmond papers, containing the dreadful details already given.

The general, taking a kindly interest in the fate of the young soldier, addressed a note to the enemy's exchange commissioner, requesting that his remains might be delivered to his father.

General Kilpatrick, who was also at the fort, called upon the admiral, and, among other statements in regard to the expedition, assured him of the falsity of the *orders* said to have been found upon his son.

The Union papers, meanwhile, abounded with

notices of the lamented martyr, expressing sorrow for his untimely end, and indignation at the conduct of the rebel authorities.

On the 23d of March, the enemy's commissioner sent word that the only officer who knew the place of interment was absent, and therefore it had been impossible to comply with the request for the body, but that this officer had been sent for.

On the 29th, the admiral again, and for the fourth time, repaired to Fortress Monroe, in order to attend personally to the reception of his son's remains, which were expected in the exchange-boat, but he was again doomed to bitter disappointment.

Arriving at home, an entire stranger called and hinted at some information, which he said had reached him, to the effect that the remains of Colonel Dahlgren had been found and removed by some friends to a place of safety, but that great secrecy was necessary, to avoid the search of the rebel authorities.

This was confirmed by a telegram from General Butler, of April 17th, stating the return of the exchange-steamer from Richmond, and that the enemy's commissioner had assured the Union commissioner, "That upon going to the grave of Colonel Dahlgren it was found empty, and that the most vigorous and persistent search fails to find it; that the authorities are making every exertion to find the body, which shall be restored if found."

It being certain that for the present no recovery would be possible, it was decided that the address which had been prepared for the funeral service should be delivered. This sad duty properly belonged to the Rev. Dr. Sunderland, as the pastor of the church in which Ulric Dahlgren had been trained, and where it was his custom to attend when at home.

No one could be so well qualified for the task as this excellent divine, who had ever been a fearless advocate of the Union cause, in season and out of season. He had personally known Ulric Dahlgren for many years, having seen him almost daily (as he passed to the church in the regular performance of his duties), most frequently near the paternal home, in some boyish recreation, or perhaps on the way to school, satchel in hand. On Sundays, too, he found the lad at his place at the Sunday-school, and afterwards, in his father's pew, a quiet and attentive listener. All who know Dr. Sunderland, are acquainted with the earnest enthusiasm with which he pursues his object, and the brilliant powers of logic and language with which he is gifted, and can well imagine the fervent feelings which animated him when he rose in the pulpit to fulfill his mission. The spacious church* was crowded to its utmost capacity, by a sympathizing

* First Presbyterian, Four-and-a-half Street.

audience gathered from every class of the community. The reverend preacher, aroused to his greatest power, held the large assembly in rapt attention for more than two hours, in the delivery of a sermon which, for accuracy of statement, pathos, and eloquence, has never been excelled, if measured by the effect on such numbers of clear, strong, earnest, and well-educated minds. The sound of the last sentence had scarcely died out when several gentlemen rose, and, speaking in behalf of those around, requested that the discourse should be printed.

This was succeeded next day, in a more formal manner, by a written application, as follows:

"WASHINGTON, D.C., April 25, 1864.

"REV. BYRON SUNDERLAND, D.D.

"DEAR SIR,—We respectfully request that you will furnish for publication a copy of the eloquent and patriotic discourse on the life and death of Colonel Dahlgren, delivered last evening. We wish to see the noble, daring, and heroic devotion to the cause of his country, which characterized the brief but brilliant career of this young soldier, held up before the youth of our country, that they may be stimulated to an honorable emulation of his virtues, and, if need be, to a similar sacrifice of their lives. We wish to honor his memory, by publishing the story of his deeds and his death, that it may go down to posterity with the record of many other noble young men of our land, whose lives have honored and whose deaths have rendered doubly sacred the cause in which they fell, and will add to the reproach and shame of all our enemies and all who sympathize with them.

"In thus presenting this request, we believe that we express the general sentiment of those who listened to your discourse, and the loyal people of this community.

"Very respectfully, your obedient servants,

"SCHUYLER COLFAX,
J. K. MOREHEAD,
D. MORRIS,
Z. D. GILMAN,
WM. H. CAMPBELL,
WM. GUNTON,
O. C. WIGHT,
MARSHALL CONANT."

To this request, the Rev. Dr. Sunderland made the following reply:

"WASHINGTON, April 26, 1864.

"TO MESSRS. SCHUYLER COLFAX, J. K. MOREHEAD, D. MORRIS, AND OTHERS.

"GENTLEMEN,—Your request of the 25th instant, so kindly expressed, is duly received; and in submitting to your disposal a copy of the discourse delivered by me, in memory of the late Colonel

Dahlgren, permit me to add, that when our countrymen shall read the story of this noble young soldier, and the nation's heart shall thrill again on every recollection of his exploits, I pray them to remember it is not upon the ground of his lofty patriotism, but upon the humble hope of his confidence in the Redeemer of the world, that his pastor cherishes the conviction of his now beatified and exalted estate, in the presence of God and the holy angels.

"Ever truly, etc.,

"B. SUNDERLAND."

It is not to be forgotten that the circumstances attending the delivery of this address were most remarkable. Its subject was personally known to most of those present, who were the neighbors of his family, and he was generally known to the congregation as one of its youth. The head of the academy where Ulric Dahlgren had been trained for some ten years, and who also had been his Sunday-school teacher, was present, as an elder of the church, and was one of those who requested the publication of the sermon. So that there was a mass of living testimony to the life and character of the gallant young soldier, that few have been favored with. These witnesses could scan nearly the whole of the brief life, had been cognizant of it in nearly every phase, and now that it was stilled forever, they could, within the sanctuary, bear evidence to its purity, its loveliness, its fidelity, courage, and great promise.

The very words themselves came from the lips and the heart of a speaker, made holy, by his devoted zeal for religion and the cause of his country, and who was himself a testimony to nearly all that he uttered.

Altogether, it was a fitting memorial to the young warrior, and wheresoever might be laid the frail tenement which his brave spirit once animated, this gave imperishable remembrance to him.

Some two days later, Admiral Dahlgren received positive information of the removal of his son's remains from Richmond to a spot unknown to the rebel government, but still within their lines. This made it unadvisable to attempt its transference North, until the flag of the Union should wave over the place.

He was thus compelled reluctantly to forego, for the present, the melancholy satisfaction of having his son's remains properly interred, and felt obliged to yield to the wishes of the Department, that he should resume his command of the South Atlantic squadron, for which he departed on the 28th of April, 1864.

Such a character, and such a career, so sadly ended, could not fail to make an impression on the public mind far beyond the limits of domestic life

Various notices appeared in the public prints, in prose and in verse. Sometimes they were addressed in condolence to the father of the gallant dead, and bear evidence of the feeling occasioned in different parts of the country by the untimely end of Ulric Dahlgren.

Some of the kindly tributes have been collected, and will be found at the close of this narrative.

The Volunteer Howitzer Company of Philadelphia, with which Ulric had been associated before the rebellion, did not forget their comrade:

"PHILADELPHIA, March, 1864.

"ADMIRAL DAHLGREN.

"SIR,—At a special meeting of the Dahlgren Howitzer Battery, Captain E. Spencer Miller commanding, held at the armory, No. 808 Market Street, on Thursday the 17th instant, the following resolutions were read, and, on motion, unanimously adopted:

"*Whereas*, Our late lieutenant, Ulric Dahlgren, after severing his connection with us, and entering the active service of his country, showed on every occasion those high qualities of courage, coolness, and warm patriotism which we so well knew and appreciated, and, after gaining promotion with a rapidity which proved his extraordinary merit, lately lost his life whilst gallantly leading his men to the very gates of Richmond, to release our fellow-citizens from rebel prisons;

"*Resolved*, That in his death the country has lost one of its most promising officers and most daring and self-denying patriots.

"*Resolved*, That not in hope of adding to the honor of one whose glory is now part of the history and treasure of his country, and whose praises are on every tongue, but to impress upon ourselves his bright example, we make this record to his memory.

"*Resolved*, That as COLONEL ULRIC DAHLGREN had, from his parentage, ties to this city and this city to him, our fellow-citizens should not be unmindful of his memory, but should raise a monument to him more permanent than mere expressions of admiration and respect.

"*Resolved*, That we will wear a badge of mourning for six months, and cause these resolutions to be published, and a copy thereof to be sent to the father of the deceased.

"Extract from the minutes.

"(Signed) CHAS. WILLING HARE,
" *Chairman pro tem.*

"Attest: E. S. CAMPBELL,
"*Secretary pro tem.*"

Great events were to take place before the outraged remains of Ulric Dahlgren were destined to rest with those of his family. Indeed, the rebellion itself was first to find its grave, not with the regrets of the country, but "*unwept and unhonored.*"

The rescue of Ulric Dahlgren's remains from the possession of the rebel authorities had scarcely been accomplished, when the leader of the American armies, gathering together his legions, moved directly for Richmond. In vain did the rebel general place himself in his path, and strive to delay or avert the fatal purpose. GRANT, steadfastly keeping the end in view, moved forward, never refusing battle when offered, and never turning from a chance to strike; so that in good season he was at the portals of the city of dungeons, and there fixed a grip on the very throat of the rebellion that was not to be relaxed whilst it had life.

Meanwhile, glorious SHERMAN had entered Atlanta; his maddened enemy, driven to hopeless despair by repeated defeat, threw himself like a tiger upon the communications of the Union army, thinking perhaps thus to shake the purpose of his antagonist.

"*Quem Deus vult perdere, prius dementat.*"

That insane movement sealed the fate of *secession*, like the crash of doom, just when our impatient public was verging to lack of faith in the decree of justice. Sherman, with rapid glance, saw his opportunity. Gathering all his force and trains into one compact mass, he swooped, like an eagle, for the ocean, dividing the power of the untouched States with fatal blow, for his magnificent conception instantly divined the result. Rebellion had ignorantly placed its head upon the block, and the avenging sword fell like light.

That march of Sherman's will ever stand on the record with the greatest achievements of war.

Moving steadily on, the general came near the great sea early in December. A single obstacle in the way, in the shape of a fort (McAllister), was brushed away by an instant stroke, and Sherman, with characteristic celerity, stepped into a small bateau and first presented himself to the expectant fleet. On the 14th of December, he and Admiral Dahlgren met in the waters of Wassaw Sound, and his presence was greeted by the ships of war with every token of welcome,—the seamen mounted the rigging and cheered, while the great cannon thundered deep base to their voices.

The fall of Savannah followed quickly, and the Christmas of 1864 was celebrated in that city, and for the first time in several years, under the folds of the national banner.

As soon as the army was sufficiently recruited and its supplies renewed, Sherman recommenced his march, taking a line sufficiently near the coast to sever the communications of the enemy's strongholds seaward. As a consequence, the insurgents were compelled to abandon the seacoast as he advanced, being hemmed seaward by the fleet, and the small body of troops that had occupied positions on the sea-islands.

Admiral Dahlgren and General Schimmelfennig entered Charleston on the 17th of February.

Early in April, Sherman was in communication with Grant, and the enemy's capital was abandoned to its fate by Lee's army, which, soon after, was also compelled to surrender to the conquerors.

Thus ended the most needless resistance to lawful authority that has ever darkened the annals of man, but in its death-struggle basely stole the life of the good President, who had so ably conducted the fortunes of the republic through the terrible vicissitudes of a bloody war.

The blood of the martyr consecrated the labor of the patriot.

The tragedy of the rebellion closed fittingly with the work of the assassin.

Immediately on the accession of peace, the remains of Ulric Dahlgren were taken to Washington, from the spot where they had reposed quietly for a whole year, beneath the green sod of the valley, far away from the desecration of a bitter foe, and only awaiting the hour when broken hearts and Christian rites should consign the heroic dead to the last, last resting-place.

The spot thus hallowed by such association is some ten miles from Richmond, on the farm of Mr. Robert Orrick, and but a short distance from the railroad. The removal thither had been effected by

Mr. Lohman, a resident of Richmond, but friendly to the Union cause and in communication with General Butler; he had been assisted by Mr. Rowley, and a few others were cognizant of the transaction.

Towards the end of June, the condition of public affairs on the Southern Atlantic coast permitted the withdrawal of the principal part of the United States naval forces, which, conformably to the directions of the Navy Department, were nearly all sent North. The admiral himself soon after arrived at Washington in the Pawnee. He lost no time in having proper examination made, in order to verify the remains of his lamented son. The intense heat of the weather, however, rendered it unadvisable to attempt their transference to the burial lot of the family, near Philadelphia. The obsequies were therefore necessarily postponed until cold weather.

Meanwhile, some evidences of the shocking details which attended the last moments of the heroic dead began to appear.

Various letters had reached the admiral at different times from parties in Virginia, stating that the writers, or persons whom they knew, were in possession of articles taken from the body of Ulric Dahlgren, which they offered to restore on condition of receiving certain specified sums of money. The base instincts of the brutal crew that surrounded the young soldier in his last moments may be readily conceived from such offers, if, indeed, they had not been fully signified by other circumstances. The admiral was happily secured from the necessity of having to deal with these atrocious villains, who thus asked the price of blood; for the detective force, with the zeal which had characterized their operations during the war, had been on the alert in endeavoring to recover whatever had belonged to Colonel Dahlgren, and were in pursuit before those who held these relics had time to consummate their infamous traffic. These vigilant officers obtained successively, from various parties, the coat worn by Colonel Dahlgren when he fell, his watch, and the golden ring for which the finger had been so brutally severed. The artificial leg was also recovered. The coat was pierced by four bullet-holes, on the left side and rather towards the back, showing clearly that the fatal volley had been fired after he passed, and not directly at him as he approached.

A horse that he was supposed to have ridden when he charged into Hagerstown, and at the time he was wounded after the battle of Gettysburg, had been regained during the summer; but he became sick soon after reaching Washington, and died, before he could be removed to the green fields, where it was intended that he should roam free from further duty.

The horse had been conveyed to a farm in Virginia, where the attention of some of our soldiers had been attracted by hearing him spoken of as "Dahlgren." Inquiry disclosed former service, and he was at once retaken.

THE CHRISTIAN BURIAL.

On Monday, the 30th of October (1865), Admiral Dahlgren proceeded to the vault, to superintend personally the removal of the remains so precious to him. Incased in a metallic casket, just as brought from Richmond, they were transported by a military guard, under command of Captain Dempsey, to the City Hall of Washington, where they remained during the night in charge of six commissioned officers.

Next day the coffin was placed in the Council-chamber, and rested there until noon, covered by the broad folds of the banner which the youth had so well served. Upon it was laid the letter of the War Department, which has been already given,* that accompanied his commission as colonel.

The Council-chamber was filled with officers and citizens. The day was lowering, and the heavy clouds threatened rain. The troops that were to act as escort were assembled in front of the City Hall, consisting of battalions from the 10th Re-

---

* Chapter xii., page 255.

serve, 18th Regiment Hancock's Corps, and the 195th and 214th Pennsylvania, commanded by Brigadier-General Gile.

At noon the coffin was lifted by eight non-commissioned officers, who proceeded to carry it out of the building, attended, as pall-bearers, by

Brigadier-General De Witt,	Colonel Fisher,
Brigadier-General Oliphant,	Colonel Callis,
Colonel Johnson,	Colonel Johnston,
Colonel Pierce,	Colonel Foust,

with the guard of honor, consisting of

Captain Eldridge,	Captain Crouse,
Captain Preston,	Captain Burnell,
Captain Dwyer,	Captain Camp,

of the Veteran Reserve Cavalry Corps.

Close behind walked the father and the younger brother, the latter having been permitted to leave West Point for the melancholy occasion; the other brother was far distant. Last came the officers of the army and navy.

Among the numerous spectators, there must have been many who remembered Ulric Dahlgren in the full bloom of his boyhood and youth, passing the happy hours just where his cold body was now being borne to receive the last tokens of respect.

The spacious church was once more crowded to

its utmost by those who came to join in the tribute so well merited from every lover of the country. Among them were the President, with nearly all his Cabinet, the mayor of the city, and other distinguished persons.

The coffin was carried forward and placed directly before the pulpit.

Never were words from that desk listened to with greater attention than those which the Rev. Mr. Beecher uttered on that solemn occasion. The discourse has been justly considered as one of the finest efforts of that extraordinary speaker. So deeply were the feelings of his audience stirred, that even the circumstance and the place could not restrain the low demonstrations that seemed to float like gentle echoes of the orator's voice. Yet was the inanimate body of the heroic dead not more still than was the vast assembly, when the discourse, breaking away from the general character of its introduction, was turned to the theme itself, and the full, rich tones of the reverend preacher came in these words to his hearers:

"We have assembled to-day to replenish our own spirits and refresh our memory with these higher truths, by paying our homage of love and admiration to one of the youngest, purest, and noblest of the spirits this war developed, and who have saved the life of this nation by freely yielding their own.

"Could we have chosen the circumstances, should we have chosen so wisely and well for this young hero's honor, as did that Providence which *then* seemed black with woe and impenetrable in mystery, but from which now the unfolding clouds reveal the benignant purpose of a loving God? Called to public duty before he reached manhood, how suddenly he shot up by conspicuous service into notice! He earned in the field that advantage which a less noble nature might have expected to have inherited from the name and services of his father, and he was advanced not by solicitation, but by achievements; he did not chase down honors, but they held a hard race to catch and keep up with him.

"Simple in the family as a child, he flamed forth in the hour of battle like outrunning fire. His courage was not reckless impetuosity; it was concentration of honest purpose. It was full of eyes of caution; not a horse broke loose and unrestrainable, but a steed under rein and broken to the rider's will. He carried home-virtues into the camp, and gloried to give time, strength, and his life for a cause dearer to him than life.

"And the closing scenes of his visible career were worthy of a nature so elevated. Scarce yet recovered from the loss, in battle, of a leg,—from a sickness accompanying, which seemed likely to take life also,—he sought and obtained permission to join a noble expedition, full of extreme peril and yet more extreme fatigues, when he yet should have been on his couch.

"The history of the sufferings of Union prisoners in rebel prison-houses has added one more chapter to the great book of cruelty. No explanations can relieve it, and no apologies tone down its hideous picture. As we go away from it down the years of history, it will neither lose ruggedness nor gain softer tints; but, like a mountain which cannot be seen from its near base, but seems to rise and spread out as you recede, so this vast atrocity will spread black against the sky down to the end of time. There is nothing like it in the history of the world, and I trust there will never be again.

"It was a heroic purpose that fired young Dahlgren to attempt the rescue of those companions in arms from such hateful bondage. Such a sympathy with others' sufferings enabled him to forget his own.

"He mounted his saddle from his crutches. His spirit sustained his body in a ride that might well wear out a man in health and strength. That he failed to rescue our pining and tormented prisoners, we all know. None will ever know the anguish with which he must have passed by the city of cruelty and given up the rescue. He had almost completed his circuit, and was nearing a friendly refuge, when from ambush there came a bullet that brought him to the ground. As an eagle falls, he fell,—not yet slain, but pierced, helpless,—dying, with helpless wing and disheveled plumage upon the ground; but an eagle yet, with unblenching eye. Death rendered him insensible to reproach and cruelty.

"And so his life ended; nay, so his life began. The body was slain, the spirit was emancipated. His hands could do no more for his country; but his example would call a thousand hands to do more than he had ever done. No more was his slender form to be seen in the charge of battle; but his name was inspiration to unnumbered youths.

"His life multiplied itself upon every generous youth who, by his example, learned '*not to count his life dear to himself*.' Dead! He was never so royally living! We are looking upon the place where he once was; not upon him. This is but the souvenir, the remembrance of him; not the man or the hero. Once he lived subject to the need of a fleshly body; but now his example walks the earth with tireless feet, and needs no ministration of food or sleep.

"Once he dwelt in house made with hands, and only one; but now he dwells in thrice ten thousand.

"Wherever children are reared to Deity and heroism, there his example lives. Where men glow with patriotism and kindle with gratitude to those who saved this land to liberty and law, there is he who gave his life for his native land. In cities and in villages, on solitary farms and in the lumberman's forest, upon the shore and in the ship, among lowland herdsmen and among mountaineers —from the shores of the Atlantic, across the great rivers and lakes, across the mountains to the Pacific Ocean—his spirit shall brood upon the young, his example shall show men how to lose their lives and gain them forever!

"Dahlgren! The name aforetime was strange to English lips, and of sound foreign to English ears. But now it is no longer your land from which it came! It is ours; it is American. Our children shall wear it; and, as long as our history lasts, Dahlgren shall mean truth, honor, bravery, and heroic sacrifice.

"Precious dead! Dust, thou needest no pity or sympathy of us! Is the eye sunken? Who of us beholds, as thou dost, from the spheres above? Is thy hand powerless? What hand or scepter on earth is like thine for influence? Is thy heart pulseless? Nay, that surely is not dead that stirs thousands of hearts with joy and gratitude. How glorious is this deathless life, this living in death! Bear ye to its rest this precious trust. *Him* ye do not bring,—only the shackles that confined his spirit! Above you, around you, with you, goes this ransomed spirit! His sufferings are ended, but not his work. Noiseless and tireless worker, as long as the sea beats the shore, or the sun warms the soil, thou shalt live and labor in thy Master's cause.

"Where this dust shall rest, shall come pilgrims innumerable. Mothers holding their babes shall look with moist eyes upon the tablet, and silently pray that God would make their sons like him. And many a poet will fill his numbers with inspiration from his sepulchre; and many a teacher, skilled in witching fiction, shall weave his deeds into instructive story.

"But, high above all, God shall give his angels charge to watch and guard his form till the resurrection morning. Then, once more, as of yore in camp he waked when the trumpet sounded, shall he hear the trump of God, and rise to victory and immortality."

The last words were uttered, and the solemn chant of the choir, deepened by the full notes of the organ, gave relief to the strained emotions of the audience.

Nothing could surpass the impression produced by this discourse, for the cold, silent remains of him that was spoken of lay in view of all, and gave reality and life to the magnificent language of the speaker.

One of those present writes, "Mr. Beecher's oration was listened to with the most intense interest by one of the largest, most appreciative, and distinguished audiences that ever assembled to do honor to the memory of any military man during the war, and the distinguished orator repeatedly electrified that vast audience with his outbursts of impassioned eloquence. Faithful as our report is, the printed words are tame and commonplace when compared with the burning utterances which fell from the lips of the inspired speaker. It was an occasion never to be forgotten by those who were so fortunate as to be present."

The remains were once more borne along the crowded aisles, placed on the hearse, and attended with every honor to the railroad depot.

Arriving at Baltimore, a body of troops was in waiting, which, to the sad notes of the funeral dirge, formed an escort through the city.

Just before midnight, the admiral reached Philadelphia with the remains of his son, which were at once taken in charge by a guard of officers, and conveyed to the Hall of Independence. The following day, the coffin was placed in the time-honored chamber, whence issued that declaration which ranked this country in the family of recognized nationalities. It had not been long since the remains of our lamented President had lain there. How little did he foresee, when yielding to his emotion on hearing of the fate of Ulric Dahlgren, that he too should fall by a traitor's bullet!

The commanding generals of the district, Mr. Henry, the Mayor of Philadelphia, and other distinguished gentlemen were assembled in the morning. The funeral discourse was pronounced by the Rev. Dr. Wilson, one of the most learned and eloquent of our Presbyterian divines; his fine, commanding presence well graced the place and the occasion. All who listened to the classic language that flowed from his lips in feeling and earnest tones, might have felt that as he spoke he was touched by the consciousness of a reality. It had been his duty to consecrate with the first rites of the church the lifeless form that lay before him, of which he thus spoke:

"These hands sprinkled the water of baptism on his infant brow; emblem of a deeper, holier cleansing of the Spirit of God in his soul. Oh, how little I thought, in the quiet, holy stillness of that peaceful chamber, when that solemn rite was performed, and of which every witness is gone but he who is chief mourner here to-day,—how little I thought of what lay behind the veil that shut out the future! But I thank God and rejoice that the prayers then offered are to-day more than answered."

And now the lamented one is carefully lifted and carried from the hall, through the grounds in its rear, reaching the outlet on Walnut Street, where the extended lines of the soldiery salute the honored bier. A throng of people look on in profound silence, from the walks, the pavements, and the windows.

Followed by the remnant of the family, by friends, and by the military, the funeral train proceeds to Laurel Hill, taking the very road which the gallant youth had himself traversed, in dutiful attendance upon the remains of mother, and brother, and sister. Now it is his turn to be thus attended.

The cemetery is reached, the procession winds along its peaceful walks, and then halts near the place of interment. Once more, and for the last time, the heroic dead is borne by the hands of men. The light of a mellow autumnal day glows on the grass and glances amid the rustling leaves; the rich green of the foliage is darkening with the hues of the departing year, and lines of armed men are formed with military precision along the way. Everything that meets the eye is in unison with the solemnity, and not a sound breaks on the ear to divert the attention from that bier. Closely following it are the father, and brother, and the reverend speaker. Presently they stand beside the narrow dwelling in mother earth which is to receive the honored relics. The coffin has been lowered to its place, and neither movement nor sound is perceptible among the living masses that gather around.

Suddenly the preacher moves from his place,

and stands at the head of the grave. Uncovered, and with raised hand, his clear, firm voice fills the space around in solemn invocation:

"We are to-day, my friends, looking upon our graves, and thinking of the skies. There is a mightier congregation here of the dead than of the living; but there is a day coming to earth's mightiest and lowliest, when all these graves shall be opened. There shall be to all of us a resurrection. God grant it may be a resurrection to life!"

The profound silence is broken only by the quick, clear click of muskets, and then comes the loud volley from a thousand muskets, repeated again and again.

They will not arouse that sleeper now; for he sleeps his last sleep.

Once, that sharp rattle would have awakened every pulse of the gallant heart that now heeds not its summons. And oh! there was *one hour* of life—the very last—when the presence of that array would have turned away death, or consecrated it with victory. But how vain such thought!

And thus honor is done to whom honor is due; even vengeance could not avert it. The noble youth at last sleeps quietly, the sleep that knows no waking. He is placed close by the mortal remains of the cherished mother, who so often moulded his young thought and brought gladness to his heart, and light to his eye. She, at least, was spared the sorrow of these hours.

In a brief space all have dispersed, and left the dead to the solitude of the grave,—their slumbers soothed by the murmuring breeze and the sound of the moving waters of the river that winds by.

Peace to his ashes! The laurels on the young and fair brow will never fade while there are true men and women in the land to keep them green.

Remembered among those the nation mourns, will be the name of Ulric Dahlgren.

APPENDIX.

A CHAPLET

FOR

ULRIC DAHLGREN.

A CHAPLET

FOR

ULRIC DAHLGREN.

DEATH OF COLONEL ULRIC DAHLGREN, UNITED STATES CAVALRY.

BY M. S. NEWCOMER.

FIRM with his face to the foe,
  Steady the sword in his hand,
Stranger to terror or woe—
  Worthy to lead such a band:
Bravely he met victory,
  Sealed with his own precious blood,
His bold heart died to be free,
  Warmed by its outgushing flood.

CHIFTAIN OF GLORY! all hail!
  Majesty pales in thy light—
Despots will stagger and quail,
  To see thee bleed for the Right:—
Freedom will sing of thy name,
  Ages of time yet to be;
Bright are the laurels of fame,
  Twining in beauty for thee.

Time will but add to the thrill,
  Swelling the popular heart,—
Vengeance and glory will still
  Blend with our tears as they start.
Garlands of roses we'll twine,
  Softly we'll speak in thine ear,
Home of the brave shall be thine,—
  Liberty weeps at thy bier!

Traitors may scoff at thy corpse,
  And fiends may howl at thy grave—
Freedom forgets not its source,
  In the warm blood of the brave.
Deity smiles upon thee;
  HERCULES OF LIBERTY! hail!—
The stripes and the stars of the free
  Will never grow languid or pale.

Treason may rave in its lair,
  Mocking the dust of the slain,
None its dark burden to bear,
  Save the brute lord of the chain;—
Liberty saved from its wrath,
  Will own the soil it has trod,
Despite the foes in its path,
  To bless its MAKER and GOD!

Village Record.

LYRICS OF TO-DAY.

FROM THE BOSTON TRANSCRIPT.

ON guard to-night—and through all the darkness comes
The notes of bugles and the roll of drums
Sounding tattoo—while from the city near—
Richmond, doomed city, trembling now with fear—
Borne on the breeze, these are the words I hear:

Who talks of peace?
Who says, Let this War cease?
While we in Libby lie and plainly hear
Brothers in arms
Sounding war's loud alarms
At Richmond's very gates, that quake with fear.

Who of peace prates
While dead and dying mates
Fill Southern graves and cells? And we all hope,—
Some for grim death,
While some, with bated breath,
Whisper of those who shall prison-doors ope.

Have ye forgot
That this accursed spot
Holds men who've bravely fought for home and you?
Day after day
They wait and watch and pray—
God grant their hopes and prayers may all come true!

For you they've borne
Insults, and taunts, and scorn,
Been robbed, and starved, and seen comrades shot dead
By prison-guards.
Are these the poor rewards
With which our country crowns the soldier's head?

Here DAHLGREN lies,
Sleeping 'neath Southern skies,
His crippled form by traitors rudely thrown
In unknown grave;
Yet there are those who rave
Of Peace, ere vengeance justly claims its own.

Ere Peace there be,
Give us our Liberty.
Let us the traitors meet once more in fight;
We all have sworn
That every wrong we've borne
Shall be wiped out in blood or in death's night.

W. H. K.

September, 1864.

ULRIC DAHLGREN.

BY REV. CHARLES W. DENISON.

WE met at Harper's Ferry, in the gorges of the hills,
Where, chasing the Potomac, come leaping down the rills;
We stood in Union armor by Shenandoah's tide,
And, ready for the battle, Sigel was by our side.
The frowning Heights of Maryland with waving plumes of gray
Through the autumnal twilight bade grand adieus that day;
The table-rocks of Jefferson gloamed in the darkness there,
And the spirit of the patriot seemed hovering in the air.

Oh, scene of desolation! The guilt, and woe, and shame
Of slavery in rebellion had burnt the land with flame;
The sleep of Justice wakened by Monticello's grave,
And in conflict with the master she sided with the slave.
In that historic temple where Washington had stood,
Before the shattered altars in old Virginia's wood,
Young DAHLGREN raised his sworded hand and sacredly he vowed,
"My country's banner shall prevail, or be my winding shroud!"

So spake the boy that evening, then dashed along the right,
And, in the name of freedom, put slavish hordes to flight;
At Fredericksburg embattled he strode the crimson field,
His watchword of the column, "To traitors never yield!"
Through the dark haze of Gettysburg he flashed a living flame,
And on the scroll of heroes wrote his own immortal name;
With the torn flag of Hagerstown his body shrouded round,
He fought oppression's myrmidons stretched bleeding on the ground;
Then torn, and maimed, and weak, he rose as valiant as of yore—
He was of age that day of grace—he was a man before.

O manful boy! O youthful peer! O Ulric the brave!
The proudest of thy patriot deeds shall monument thy grave.
Around thy hidden sod at night the grateful slave shall cling,
And in fond tones through Libby's cells thy requiem shall ring.
Almost alone, without the trump and blazonry of war,
In darkness, hand to hand with death, thou wert death's conqueror.
Above that spot our flag will float, but not thy shroud; 'twill be
The pennon call to avenge thy fall, borne over land and sea;
With Winthrop and with Lyon, with Foote and Shaw art thou,
And DAHLGREN shines with them henceforth on Freedom's starry
brow.

ALLYN HOUSE, HARTFORD.

LINES SUGGESTED BY THE DEATH OF ONE OF THE BRAVEST MEN THIS WAR HAS BROUGHT INTO THE SERVICE—

COLONEL ULRIC DAHLGREN.

ULRIC DAHLGREN, in the story
  Of thy country's grief and wrong,
Yours shall stand a name of glory,
  Bright in history and song.

Since bold treason sent its thunder
  Over Charleston's placid bay,
While the world looked on in wonder
  At the madness of the day,

Oh, how many lives have perished—
  Gone, like bubbles on the brine—
Lives by warm affection cherished—
  None, young hero, more than thine!

Thou, scarce launched on life's great ocean,
  Courage thine, both rare and grand,
Thy young heart's supreme devotion
  To thy dear, thy native land,

Joined to make all patriots love thee,
  Joined to give thee station, power—
In th' embattled field to prove thee
  Worthy, 'mid the wildest hour.

ULRIC DAHLGREN, thou hast given
  Thy blood in freedom's cause to flow;
God will bless thee up in heaven,
  Good men bless thee here below.

Traitors hate thee—oh, the glory
  Of *such* hatred to the true!
Traitor, scoundrel, villain, tory,
  Ever will hate such as you.

Sleep, young hero; thou, in dying,
  Fallest in the cause of right;
And thy memory, time defying,
  Shall be ever, ever bright.

B. B. FRENCH.

WASHINGTON, D. C.

ULRIC DAHLGREN.

BY CHARLES HENRY BROCK.

QUENCH the burning indignation,
Check the rising tear;
Be his sepulchre the Nation,
And the Land his bier!

Hellish vengeance hath consigned him
To a grave unknown:
Freedom's angel hath enshrined him
By her altar-stone.

Curse and mangle, O ye traitors!
What is left of him:
Crush and sever, ruthless haters!
Every youthful limb;

Hide him in your dark morasses,
That no verdant sod
E'er may tell, to him who passes,
Where he rests with God.

But ye cannot crush the story
Of his hero-worth,
Nor debase his wealth of glory
With ignoble earth.

And ye cannot hide the gleaming
Of his hero-name,
For it kindles with each beaming
Of his Country's fame!

Spirit of the son immortal!
  Wailings of the sire!
Peace, for in your Nation's portal
  Hangs the funeral lyre;

Breathing there the mighty chorus
  Of the young and brave,
How he died, awhile before us,
  Liberty to save!

Oh, be this the consolation,
  This the mourner's pride,
That the story fires the Nation,
  How he lived and died!

Be the sepulchre that holds him
  Hidden as it may,
'Tis his Country that enfolds him
  With her native clay.

PHILADELPHIA, March, 1864.

THE CARVED LETTERS.

AN INCIDENT IN THE BOYHOOD OF THE BRAVE YOUNG SOLDIER, COLONEL ULRIC DAHLGREN.

It was a morn of summer,
And the woods were waving free,
When a youthful group stood resting
Beneath an old beech-tree.

We had wandered through the woodland,
Had culled the modest flowers,
And watched the sweet birds flitting
Across the shaded bowers.

And now beside the streamlet,
To list its silver song,
We rested in the noontide,
For the summer days are long.

A spell seemed o'er us thown,
The air was hushed and still,
And the flowers bent down, half sleeping,
Above the singing rill.

And the dreamy hush of Nature
Laid its touch upon each brow;
All our merry converse languished,
We scarce knew why, or how.

Then a stripling, tall and slender,
Arose in quiet wise;
His brow was broad and truthful,
And earnest were his eyes.

There on the bark, moss-broidered,
That clothed the ancient tree,
He carved, with careful touches,
Two letters quaint—**U. D.**

We watched him in the stillness,
But the work was done full soon;
And our path was taken homeward
Ere the twilight's evening gloom.

We saw not, in our blindness,
What his task might typify;
For the coming years' sad record
Was veiled from mortal eye.

The sky was pure and cloudless,
The air was fresh and sweet;
The flowering grass shed perfume
As we stirred it with our feet.

And in this wealth of beauty
But *One* could truly know
That passion-fires were smouldering,
To break in pain and woe.

It came! the crash of cannon,
That shook our peaceful land,
And turned the crook and plowshare
To sword and warlike brand.

It roused the noble spirit
That dwelt within the youth;
And forth he rushed to battle
For his Country and for Truth.

No path could Duty show him
  Too hard for him to go;
But swift as wingéd lightning
  He fell upon the foe.

And by his holy daring,
  For Right, to do or die,
He carved his name ancestral
  On Honor's roll full high.

The tree may fall and perish,
  The letters there may fade;
But never shall his memory
  Be in oblivion laid.

But ever 'mid the bravest
  Shall shine in glory forth
The name of ULRIC DAHLGREN,
  The hero of the North.

M. T. C.

ON, September 16, 1864.

ULRIC DAHLGREN.

BY HENRY T. TUCKERMAN.

WHEN, circled by the fond and fair,
  We saw thee maimed and pale,
With that heroic, gentle air
  Before which cowards quail;

So radiant in the grasp of pain,
  So meek with valor's crown,
Our swelling hearts could not refrain
  To bless thy young renown.

Youth's artless cheer with manhood's thought
  In word and glance o'erflow,
As if thy life had newly caught
  Thy blood's ancestral glow;

The spirit of old Sweden's king
  Which mien and accent bore,
In every pulse-beat seemed to spring
  Intrepid as of yore.

It nerved thy arm in wild foray,
  And round thy martyr's bed,
Where love and faith still watch and pray,
  Angelic patience shed.

Vain the base ambush from whose lair
  The murderer's bullet came,
And vain the slander that would tear
  The glory from thy name.

O Ulric! brutal hate will pine,
  All impotent to sear
The laurels that thy country's shrine
  Forever shall endear.

COLONEL ULRIC DAHLGREN.

BY EPES SARGENT.

O YOUTH beloved, revered!
Now to all hearts endeared,
  Loyal and true,—
What grief profound was stirred,
When of thy fate we heard,
  'Mid the foul crew!

Not thy fifth lustrum told,
Thou wert in service old,
  Crippled and scarred;
Yet in thy boyish hand
Wielding the leader's brand,
  Honor's bright guard!

Shall we deplore thy lot,
Never to be forgot
  On history's page?
No! in immortal youth
There lift thy brow of truth
  From age to age!

No! we will weep no more;
No! we will not deplore,
  Dahlgren! thy fall:
Life-growth to freedom's tree,
Blood such as thine shall be:—
  Glorious thy call!

Let, then, from rebel throat
Issue the taunting note,
  Mocking thy fame:
That fame shall mount the higher,—
Shall all our youth inspire
  With its pure flame!

COLONEL ULRIC DAHLGREN.

FROM THE SPRINGFIELD WEEKLY REPUBLICAN, APRIL 9, 1864.

SENTRY stand the Southern pines,
Tenderly the moonlight shines,
Where the mould hath hidden deep
Hero-dust where none may weep;
Ever towards that lonely glen
Turn the hearts of Northern men;
Voices 'neath a Southern sky
Breathe a name that cannot die,—
DAHLGREN!

Well we know that midnight dread—
Baffled, broken, and misled—
When glad hope and courage high
Meant—"a dog's death" there to die!
Well we know how bravely then
Stood thy band of death-doomed men,
With the prowling wolves atrack,
Home and friends behind their back,
DAHLGREN!

Patriot-martyr, not in vain
Poured thy breast its crimson rain!
Hero-blood makes noble seed!
Pity, in their hour of need,
Those who hear that name again
On the lips of earnest men,
With the death-stern battle-cry,
Front to front, and eye to eye,
DAHLGREN!

THE

WORKS OF WASHINGTON IRVING.

EDITIONS OF IRVING'S WORKS.

I. The Knickerbocker Edition.—Large 12*mo, on* superfine laid, tinted paper. Profusely Illustrated with Steel Plates and Wood-cuts, elegantly printed from new stereotype plates. Complete in 27 vols. Bound in extra cloth, gilt top. Per vol. $2.50. Half calf, gilt extra. Per vol. $4.

*II. The Riverside Edition.—*16*mo, on fine white* paper; from new stereotype plates. With Steel Plates. Complete in 26 vols. Green crape cloth, gilt top, beveled edges. Per vol. $1.75. Half calf, gilt extra. Per vol. $3.25.

*III. The People's Edition.—From the same stereo*type plates as above, but printed on cheaper paper. Complete in 26 vols. 16mo. With Steel Vignette Titles. Neatly bound in cloth. Per vol. $1.25. Half calf neat. Per vol. $2.50.

*IV. The Sunnyside Edition.—*12*mo, on fine toned* paper. With Steel Plates. Complete in 28 vols. Handsomely bound in dark-green cloth. Per vol. $2.25. Half calf, gilt extra. Per vol. $4.

Embracing the following:

Bracebridge Hall,	Goldsmith,	Granada,
Wolfert's Roost.	Alhambra,	Salmagundi,
Sketch Book,	Columbus, 3 vols.,	Spanish Papers, 2 vols.
Traveler,	Astoria,	Washington, 5 vols.,
Knickerbocker,	Bonneville,	Life and Letters, 4 vols.
Crayon Miscellany,	Mahomet, 2 vols.,	

The reissue of these works in their several forms is unusually elegant. The plates are new, the paper superior, the printing handsome, and each, in proportion to price, combining good taste with economy.

☞ **EACH WORK SOLD SEPARATELY.** ☜

LIPPINCOTT'S PRONOUNCING DICTIONARY

OF

BIOGRAPHY AND MYTHOLOGY

Containing Memoirs of the Eminent persons of all Ages and Countries and Accounts of the Various Subjects of the Norse, Hindoo and Classic Mythologies, with the Pronunciation of their Names in the different Languages in which they occur. By J. THOMAS, A. M., M. D. Imperial 8vo. Published in Parts of 64 pages. Price 50 cents per Part. In two handsome vols. Per vol., extra cloth, $11. Sheep, $12. Half Turkey, $13.50.

This invaluable work embraces the following peculiar features to an eminent degree:

I. GREAT COMPLETENESS AND CONCISENESS IN THE BIOGRAPHICAL SKETCHES.

II. SUCCINCT BUT COMPREHENSIVE ACCOUNTS OF ALL THE MORE INTERESTING SUBJECTS OF MYTHOLOGY.

III. A LOGICAL SYSTEM OF ORTHOGRAPHY.

IV. THE ACCURATE PRONUNCIATION OF THE NAMES.

V. FULL BIBLIOGRAPHICAL REFERENCES.

"I have taken the trouble to look out a large number of names, such as seemed to me good tests of the compass, sufficency and accuracy of the biographical notices. The result has been in a high degree satisfactory. So far as I have examined nobody was omitted that deserved a place, and the just proportions were maintained between the various claimants to their page, or paragraph, or line. The star of the first magnitude was not shorn of its radiance, and the scarcely visible spark was allowed its little glimmer."—*From* DR. OLIVER WENDELL HOLMES.

"It is a work which I shall be glad to possess, both on account of the fullness of its matter, and because the pronunciation of the names is given. I have had occasion, from the other works of Dr. Thomas, to be convinced of his great exactness in that respect. The work will be a valuable addition to the books of reference in our language."—*From* WILLIAM CULLEN BRYANT.

"I can speak in high terms of the thoroughness and accuracy with which the work has been prepared. It is a storehouse of valuable and trustworthy information. The pronunciation of the names, which is systematically given, will add much to the usefulness of the work."—*From Prof.* JAMES HADLEY, *Yale College.*

"I think that the work when completed will supply a real want. I was especially pleased with the sensible and learned preface of the editor, and am persuaded that he has chosen the true system of orthography. From what I know of Dr. Thomas, I feel sure that he will give us a book that may be depended on for comprehensiveness and accuracy, the two great *desideranda* in such an undertaking."—*From Prof.* JAS. RUSSELL LOWELL.

"It is the most valuable work of the kind in English that I have seen."—*From* GEN. R. E. LEE, *Washington College.*

Special Circulars, containing a full description of the work, with specimen pages, will be sent, post-paid, on application.

Subscriptions received by the Publishers, and the Parts forwarded to subscribers by mail, post-paid, as issued, on receipt of the price (50 cents) for each part.

Agents wanted in all parts of the United States on liberal terms. Address the Publishers.

PRESCOTT'S WORKS.

CROWN OCTAVO EDITION.

COMPLETE IN FIFTEEN UNIFORM VOLUMES.

EACH VOLUME WITH PORTRAIT ON STEEL.

Prescott's History of the Reign of Ferdinand and Isabella the Catholic. Three vols. 8vo.

Prescott's Biographical and Critical Miscellanies. With a finely engraved steel Portrait of the Author. One vol. 8vo.

Prescott's History of the Conquest of Mexico, with a Preliminary View of the Ancient Mexican Civilization, and the Life of the Conqueror, Fernando Cortez. In three vols. 8vo.

Prescott's History of the Reign of Philip the Second, King of Spain. In three vols. 8vo.

Prescott's History of the Conquest of Peru, with a Preliminary View of the Civilization of the Incas. In two vols. 8vo.

Prescott's Robertson's History of the Reign of the Emperor Charles the Fifth. With an account of the Emperor's Life after his Abdication. In three vols. 8vo.

Each work sold separately. Price per vol., cloth, $2.50; half calf, neat, $3.75; half calf, gilt extra, marble edges, $4.25; half Turkey, gilt top, $4.50. Complete sets, printed on tinted paper, handsomely bound in green or claret-colored cloth, gilt top, beveled boards. Price, $40.

CHAMBERS'S BOOK OF DAYS.

The Book of Days: A Miscellany of Popular Antiquities in connection with the Calendar, including Anecdote, Biography and History, Curiosities of Literature, and Oddities of Human Life and Character. In two vols. royal 8vo. Price per set, cloth, $9; sheep, $10; half Turkey, $11. Edited under the supervision of ROBERT CHAMBERS.

This work consists of

I.—Matters connected with the Church Calendar, including the Popular Festivals, Saints' Days, and other Holidays, with illustrations of Christian Antiquities in general.

II.—Phenomena connected with the Seasonal Changes.

III.—Folk-Lore of the United Kingdom: namely, Popular Notions and Observances connected with Times and Seasons.

IV.—Notable Events, Biographies and Anecdotes connected with the Days of the Year.

V.—Articles of Popular Archæology, of an entertaining character tending to illustrate the progress of Civilization, Manners, Literature and Ideas in those kingdoms.

VI.—Curious, Fugitive and Inedited Pieces.

The work is printed in a new, elegant and readable type and illustrated with an abundance of Wood Engravings.

www.ingramcontent.com/pod-product-compliance
Lightning Source LLC
LaVergne TN
LVHW020229110826
845151LV00003B/866

* 9 7 8 1 4 2 5 5 3 1 0 0 3 *